STOP THE

MADNESS

Finding Freedom from

ADDICTIONS

PICKINGUP
THE PIECES

by Ben Colter and Dr. Paul Hardy

Stop the Madness: Finding Freedom from Addictions
© 2006 Serendipity House

Published by Serendipity House Publishers
Nashville, Tennessee

ISBN: 1-5749-4187-9

Dewey Decimal Classification: 616.8
Subject Headings: COMPULSIVE BEHAVIOR \ TWELVE-STEP PROGRAM \
BEHAVIOR MODIFICATION

To purchase additional copies of this resource or other studies:
ORDER ONLINE at www.SerendipityHouse.com;
WRITE Serendipity House, 117 10th Avenue North, Nashville, TN 37234
FAX (615) 277-8181   PHONE (800) 525-9563

1-800-525-9563
www.SerendipityHouse.com

Printed in the United States of America

12 11 10 09 08 07 06   1 2 3 4 5 6 7 8 9 10

CONTENTS

WHY THE 12 STEPS?

In *Stop The Madness* we're are going to combine several approaches with the goal of ending our addiction and compulsions. This resource provides a fresh approach to finding healing and freedom from the inside out. It integrates the Christian 12 Steps, with solution-focused thinking, the power of community, prayer, and the awesome power of the Holy Spirit. Why the 12 Steps?

They're time-tested and effective. Since inception, these 12 Steps have been utilized in the most universally and interculturally effective recovery programs.

They're driven by biblical principles. Each step in grounded in biblical truth.

Organized in thought, they cover all the bases. Each step builds on the others so that each person involved walks through a full cycle of recovery and ongoing freedom.

They're not just for addicts. These steps get to the root of any kind of addiction. Those of us who are addicted know that we want whatever we're searching for immediately. Working through the steps can be a help to anyone who needs to learn patience with themselves and others.

They mark a pathway for ongoing freedom in Christ. The ultimate goal of this series is NOT only recovery but, ongoing freedom in Christ. Rather than forcing temporary change through behavior modification, the steps focus on the heart, so we see lasting change that flows from the inside out.

EXPERIENCE RESTORATION

Another Picking Up the Pieces resource, *Pursued By God – An Experience in Redemptive Worship CD,* can encourage you on your journey to freedom. Engage your soul at the deepest level through songs of redemptive worship worship as it was meant to be ... real-time, multidirectional, intimate interaction with God Himself. It provides an opportunity to experience healing that can only come when we share our heart with God, and listen for what He wants to say to us personally.

Available from Serendipity House

You Can Be Free!

In our hearts we scream, "I just want to be free!"

We all want to be free—to really enjoy life. None of us likes dealing with the pain and emptiness in our lives. Our desire to find meaning, significance, belonging, adventure, and close relationships send us searching. But too often we turn to the wrong things to numb the pain or escape for just a little while. Even Christians are not immune. So, how did we end up trapped and powerless over our addictions?

It begins with an overwhelming sense that something has taken over and we just can't get the controls back. "I just can't stop!" Yet, we have to understand that God never meant for us to live this way, a life unmanageable and out of control. He wants us to be free!

> *It was for freedom that Christ set us free; therefore keep standing firm and do not be subject again to the yoke of slavery.* (Galatians 5:1)

But we're not free! While we experience brief times of enjoyment, it never lasts and our deepest thirsts are never quenched. Our "drug of choice" eventually just sucks us deeper and deeper into pain, isolation, shame, and captivity to the very thing we turned to for help.

Addictions come in all shapes and sizes. Our "drug of choice" might be anything: spending, alcohol, drugs, pornography, affairs, food, people, jobs, even Christian service. They touch that part of our heart created for deep communion with God, offering enjoyment, relief from pain, or fulfillment, but they come with chains of bondage. These counterfeit lovers grab our hearts, demanding more and more, but never quenching our deepest thirsts.

Jesus longs for us to be free. He knows all about our past, our hurts, our destructive habits, and our addictions. He wants to set you free from all that. Jesus alone can heal our pain and fill our hearts with the one thing we were born searching for. Jesus' mission, explained in Isaiah 61:1-3, shows how much Jesus longs for each of us to be free:

> *He sent me to bind up the brokenhearted, to proclaim freedom for the captives and release from darkness for the prisoners, to proclaim the year of the LORD's favor and the day of vengeance of our God, to comfort all who mourn, to provide for those who grieve in Zion—to bestow on them the crown of beauty instead of ashes, the oil of gladness instead of mourning, and a garment of praise instead of a spirit of despair.*

We can access divinely powerful resources! *Stop The Madness* is a life-changing group resource with a fresh, transforming approach to the time-tested 12 Step process. Real, lasting change comes from the inside out. With a community of fellow strugglers, using divinely powerful resources, we can stop the insanity and experience freedom!

12 Steps to Recovery*

Starting with Decision

1. Admit your Need (We can't do it on our own): We admit that life has become unmanageable, and that we're powerless over our addictions, compulsive behavior, and life direction.

   I know that nothing good lives in me, that is, in my flesh. For the desire to do what is good is with me, but there is no ability to do it. — Romans 7:18 HCSB

2. Find New Power (Hope to stop the madness): We embrace the truth that it requires a Power greater than ourselves to restore us to sanity, and to set us free.

   The weapons we fight with are not the weapons of this world. On the contrary, they have divine power to demolish strongholds. — 2 Corinthians 10:4 NIV

3. Make a Decision (The power to choose ... use it!): We make a decision to choose life, and to turn our lives and our wills over to the care of God more and more as we know Him deeper.

   Therefore, I urge you, brothers, in view of God's mercy, to offer your bodies as living sacrifices, holy and pleasing to God—this is your spiritual act of worship. — Romans 12:1 NIV

Searching My Self

4. Take Inventory (The DNA of our addictions): We make a searching and fearless inventory of our lives and our hearts ... to map the DNA of our addictions.

   Let us examine and probe our ways, and let us return to the Lord. Lamentations 3:40 NASB

5. Admit your addiction to Others (Break the power of secrecy): We admit to God, ourselves, and another human being the exact nature of our failures, and the burdens we've been carrying alone.

   Therefore, confess your sins to one another and pray for one another so that you may be healed. — James 5:16 HCSB

6. Prepare for Change (New things have come): We become entirely ready to have God forgive, restore, and redeem our lives, and help us live out of the new desires of our new heart.

   If anyone is in Christ, he is a new creation; the old has gone, the new has come. — 2 Corinthians 5:17 NIV

* NOTE: These 12 Steps were modified from the Alcoholics Anonymous steps

SEEKING HEALING & CHANGE

7. INVITE GOD TO RESTORE & REDEEM YOUR LIFE (A change of heart & mind): We humbly ask Jesus to correct our wrong beliefs, and to change our lives from the inside out.

Do not conform any longer to the pattern of this world, but be transformed by the renewing of your mind. Then you will be able to test and approve what God's will is. – ROMANS 12:2 NIV

8. IDENTIFY RESENTMENTS AND OFFENSES (In harm's way): We make a list of all the people we've harmed, and those who have harmed us. Then, we determine to make amends to them all.

See to it that no one misses the grace of God and that no bitter root grows up to cause trouble and defile many. – HEBREWS 12:15 NIV

9. MAKE AMENDS (Getting beyond regrets): We make direct amends to people we've harmed whenever possible, except when to do so would injure them or others.

If you are offering your gift on the altar and there you remember that your brother has something against you, leave your gift there in front of the altar. First go and be reconciled with your brother, and then come and offer your gift. – MATTHEW 5:23-24 HCSB

STICKING WITH IT

10. BE PREVENTATIVE (Relapse prevention): We continue to take personal inventory, and proactively live out of our new heart. When we are wrong, we promptly admit it, and turn back to truth and light.

Let him who thinks he stands take heed that he does not fall. – 1 CORINTHIANS 10:12 NASB

11. STAY CONNECTED WITH GOD (Keeping God in my story): We seek through listening prayer, Bible study, and heart transformation, to keep improving our relationship with God, seeking His presence, direction, and power in our lives..

Jesus said ... "If you continue in My word, you really are My disciples. You will know the truth, and the truth will set you free." – JOHN 8:31-32 HCSB

12. SHARE YOUR STORY OF REDEMPTION (Setting captives free): Having experienced a spiritual awakening as the result of these steps, we begin to carry this message of hope and healing to others, as we continue to apply the steps in every area of our lives.

He [God], comforts us in all our affliction, so we may be able to comfort those who are in any kind of affliction, through the comfort we ourselves receive from God. 2 CORINTHIANS 1:4 HCSB

GROUP MEETING STRUCTURE

Each of your group meetings will include a four-part agenda.

(1) BREAKING THE ICE:
This section includes fun, uplifting questions to warm up the group and help group members get to know one another better, as they begin the journey of becoming a connected community. These questions prepare the group for meaningful discussion throughout the session.

(2) DISCOVERING THE TRUTH:
The heart of each session is the interactive Bible study time. The goal is for the group to discover biblical truths through open, discovery questions that lead to further investigation. The emphasis in this section is two-fold: (1) to provide instruction about the process of recovery and freedom; and (2) understand what the Bible says through interaction within your group.

NOTE: To help the group experience a greater sense of community, it is important for everybody to participate in the "Discovering the Truth" and "Embracing the Truth" discussions. Even though people in a group have differing levels of biblical knowledge, it is vital that group members encourage each other share what they are observing, thinking, and feeling about the Bible passages.

(3) EMBRACING THE TRUTH:
All study should direct group members to action and life change. This section continues the Bible study time, but with an emphasis on leading group members toward integrating the truths they have discovered into their lives. The questions are very practical and application-focused.

(4) CONNECTING:
One of the key goals of this study to lead group members to grow closer to one another as the group develops a sense of community. This section focuses on further application, as well as opportunities for encouraging, supporting, and praying for one another.

TAKING IT HOME:
Between each session, there is some homework for group members. This may include a question to take to God, a question to take to your heart, questions about your story; and activities that must be completed to continue on with your 12-Step Recovery Map. "Taking It Home" is a critical part of the recovery process.

A LOOK AT THE PATHWAY TO HEALING

BREAKING THE ICE - 20 MINUTES

> **LEADER:** *Be sure to read the introductory material in the front of this book and the Leader's material at the end of the book before the first session. Encourage everyone to participate in the "Breaking the Ice" questions. In question 4, help group members get to know one another by introducing yourself first, saying something like this, "Hi, I'm _____ I'm a grateful Christ-follower in my recovery from _____ (your specific area of recovery).*

1. Which of the following captures one of your most memorable outdoor experiences growing up?
   - ☐ Mountain Joe - "There's nothing like the fresh air and freedom of a mountain hike!"
   - ☐ Family Camping - "Camping as a family was a great way to get away from it all."
   - ☐ Friendly Fun - "We sure got into some trouble hanging out in the woods."
   - ☐ Urban Adventure - "I love to sweat it off at the gym."
   - ☐ "I was never an outdoors person, but I had a lot of fun doing _____."
   - ☐ Other - _____

2. If time and money were no object for you, what would your ideal excursion be? Who would you like to take with you?

3. Take turns introducing yourselves to each other in the group. Share your name, a little about your family and the place you grew up, and one reason you joined this group.

OPENING PRAYER:

God, we're grateful for each person that has joined us for this journey. As we take this journey together, let us have an ever-growing sense of Your presence with us. We ask that, as You protect us, heal us, comfort us, and guide us that we will develop a sense of community together in this group.

We're all on a path. Most people have never been able to define their path, they just walk through life. Others walk their path and are determined in their direction, only to find that they were actually on the wrong path! Many of us feel that we've been to hell and back, and long for someone to guide us to safer, more appropriate places. The truth is, you don't have to go it alone. You'll have several important people to help you:

Your Facilitator (Group Leader): This person will help the group stay on track. Most likely, they have already been where you'll be going. They know the twists and turns and want to help you navigate.

A Mentor: If people are available to help, your group leader may assign a mentor to you. This would be a person who has been through what you're going through, and can help to guide and encourage you too.

An Accountability Partner: Once you choose someone in the group who will encourage and challenge you, you'll see your life and struggles in a new light. This person will ask tough questions, encourage you, and help you think more objectively. An accountability partner must be the same gender, unless you struggle with homosexuality.

The Holy Spirit: Unless the Spirit of God shows up and meets with us in each session we'll only gain information. Life change and healing is the goal. If we invite God into our struggle He will guide us into truth, and that truth is vital to healing and freedom (John 8:32)!

So, how about it ... Are you ready for a journey? There are adventures, dangers, fears, challenges, and obstacles to overcome. As we take the journey to "stop the madness," we look forward to being refreshed, renewed and, most of all, forever changed!

OBJECTIVES FOR THIS SESSION:

- Discover the power in community and key values for healing and recovery
- Understand how this study is applicable to an array of addictions and out-of-control behaviors
- Put our addictions and experiences into biblical context
- Become familiar with the concepts and purpose of the 12 Steps (on pages 6-7)
- Introduce the Group Covenant

DISCOVERING THE TRUTH - 25 MINUTES

KEY VALUES FOR RECOVERY

¹ Therefore since we also have such a large cloud of witnesses surrounding us, let us lay aside every weight and the sin that so easily ensnares us, and run with endurance the race that lies before us, ² keeping our eyes on Jesus, the source and perfecter of our faith, who for the joy that lay before Him endured a cross and despised the shame, and has sat down at the right hand of God's throne. ³ For consider Him who endured such hostility from sinners against Himself, so that you won't grow weary or lose heart.

HEBREWS 12:1-3 HCSB

(1) THE POWER OF "REDEMPTIVE COMMUNITY":

1. Who do you think the author of Hebrews is referring to here? How might they be a powerful resource in overcoming your addictions?

NOTE: The imagery used is that of an athlete standing in the middle of the great stadium in Rome or another city, and looking high up at the cheering crowds that blended with the sky. For us, those who've gone before us are cheering us on saying, "You can do it! You are more than you realize!" We are also called to cheer for one another. This is an essential element in the healing process.

Confess your sins to one another and pray for one another, so that you may be healed. The intense prayer of the righteous is very powerful.

JAMES 5:16 HCSB

No! conflict of
Shots #5

2. What does James 5:16 encourage us to do? How could we apply this within the context of this group?

God calls us to be a "Redemptive Community" Not just any community, but a community of people He can work through to redeem our messes (see Joel 2:25). We have come to seek healing together. This is a safe place. Safety means you can be yourself, and tell your story without the fear of ridicule or shame. This group should be a model for healthy community. As each of us tells our story we are able to invite God into the process of redeeming what we've lost. Recovery simply means we're banding together as redeemed (recovered) individuals journeying toward healing, freedom, and wholeness.

(2) SENSITIVITY TO RELAPSE:

3. Why might the author of Hebrews allow for no moderation when it comes to dealing with (laying aside) stuff that can trip us up or ensnare us?

God takes freedom from addictions very seriously ... we need to be practical and sensitive to the possibility of relapse. If you line up to run in a race, you don't put on an overcoat with large rocks in all the pockets. You strip off every weight. It's time to strip off the weights that hold us down in our race, our struggles. It's all about our deepest beliefs and choices. Our beliefs drive our choices that form the habit patterns we come to repeat.

(3) STOPPING THE MADNESS:

4. The writer of Hebrews reveals a level of intense focus and concentration in verses 2-3. Why is focus so important to your recovery?

Recovery will require focus. Anything that gets between you, God, and your recovery is something that needs to removed. Some of us may need to detox. We may need to abstain, turn away from, remove ourselves from the people, places, or things that trigger the actions we are here to overcome.

(4) SETTING OUR SIGHTS ON "THE ONE" WHO CAN HEAL US!

5. Why would "keeping our eyes on Jesus" be so important to any recovery process?

There IS a Higher Power and His name is Jesus. We become "like" the object of our attention. That's why we might hear, "You're more like your father every day." Jesus really understands <u>suffering</u> and <u>struggles</u> ... and He has the power to overcome them!

The key to change is our focus! In addictions, our problem is that we become problem-focused. We stare at the problem and don't see any solutions. We need to become convinced that there's a solution to every problem. Now, that brings hope! Here's the solution: focus on Jesus. When we put Him in the center of our lives, we are forever changed! You can be free!

AM I THE ONLY ONE THAT'S MESSED UP?

In a word ... NO.

> **LEADER:** *Read the following summaries and ask the questions of the group. Ask for volunteers to read the Bible passages aloud. Become very familiar with the passages and be prepared to answer any questions or objections. Some members may be prepared to share their ideas with the group. Others may be quiet and reserved until they feel like they fit into the group. Try to even out the discussion by inviting various people to answer; don't allow any one person to dominate the time.*

We all experience pain and emptiness at times in our lives. The problem is that we often turn to the wrong things to numb the pain or escape for a while. We might experience some brief times of enjoyment, but it never lasts. Those things eventually just suck us deeper and deeper into pain and isolation.

So, can a person be completely engulfed in a behavior that they've justified in their thinking, believing they are totally in the right, and yet be completely mistaken in their direction? That's the story of Saul's life. He was the most dedicated guy around. He meant well. He was consumed by an inner drive, a desire to somehow please God. There was a simple problem: he was unmistakably walking down the wrong path! Check it out.

Paul

A Driven Man on the Damascus Road

[1] *Meanwhile Saul, still breathing threats and murder against the disciples of the Lord, went to the high priest* [2] *and requested letters from him to the synagogues in Damascus, so that if he found any who belonged to the Way, either men or women, he might bring them as prisoners to Jerusalem.* [3] *As he traveled and was nearing Damascus, a light from heaven suddenly flashed around him.* [4] *Falling to the ground, he heard a voice saying to him, "Saul, Saul, why are you persecuting Me?"*
[5] *"Who are You, Lord?" he said.*

"I am Jesus, whom you are persecuting," He replied. [6] *"But get up and go into the city, and you will be told what you must do."*
[7] *The men who were traveling with him stood speechless, hearing the sound but seeing no one.* [8] *Then Saul got up from the ground, and though his eyes were open, he could see nothing. So they took him by the hand and led him into Damascus.* [9] *He was unable to see for three days, and did not eat or drink.*

ACTS 9:1-9 HCSB

6. What was it that Saul was driven to do (verses 1-2)? How do you think his actions affected other people? How did his actions affect Jesus who had already returned to heaven (verses 4-5)?

7. Saul was a driven man. Can you relate to his drive? What do you believe might have been at the heart of is drivenness?

8. Describe the most driven person you've ever observed (a friend, relative, professional who never counted time or energy spent on a project, inventors who never took care of themselves, etc.). How did this drivenness or addiction affect his or her life?

EMBRACING THE TRUTH - 25 MINUTES

LEADER: *"Embracing the Truth" is the section in each meeting where group members will begin to integrate the truth they're discovering into their personal lives. Be aware that everybody is in a different place in their struggles, so the rate of life application will vary ... and that's okay.*

1. It took a personal intervention by God to free Saul from his drivenness. He was literally knocked to the ground. What do you think it would take to get your full and undivided attention? Has that happened yet?

2. In this encounter with Jesus, what question and answer began to free Saul from his drivenness (see verse 5)?

12 Steps to Recovery

In a moment in the presence of Christ, all of Saul's inner stuff and true beliefs were called out by Jesus. Then, through a process of years, God healed and retrained him. He became the Apostle Paul, a man set free to make a huge difference in the world. We, too, will walk through a process to overcome the addictions that hold us captive and control us.

> **LEADER:** *Ask group members to TURN TO PAGES 6-7 for a brief overview of the 12 Steps. Keep this brief; don't dive in now. Understanding will come in the weeks ahead. Feel free to point out the "Why the 12 Steps?" notes on PAGE 4. You may ask for volunteers to read a step or verse aloud.*
>
> **OPTION:** *Show a rope with several knots. Explain that this rope represents the path we're on. The rope is the process of recovery. The knots represent many places this journey will take us — steps and events that seal parts of our recovery in our hearts forever.*

Turn to pages 6-7 in this book to walk through a brief overview of the 12 Steps to Recovery. This will only give you some idea of the journey you're on. You'll fully understand each step as you come to it in the weeks ahead.

Connecting - 20 minutes

> **LEADER:** *This is a part of the weekly session in which you help group members begin to connect with each other, with you as their facilitator, with their own hearts, and with God. This connecting is vital for the group to grow toward becoming a Redemptive Community.*

Some people believe recovery is a one-time event. Bam! You're delivered. For some people that seems to be true. For most, recovery is a process of life-changing events. In that process, they're engaging their stories and dealing with their issues.

1. How has it been for you? Share some of the experiences you've had trying to recover on your own or through other groups or means.

LEADER INSTRUCTIONS FOR GROUP EXPERIENCE: *Show the video clip from the Disney-animated movie* The Lion King *in which Simba (the main character) says he's confused and doesn't know who he is anymore. This scene ends when the spirit of his father tells him, "You're more than you've become .... remember who you are." This clip is in scene 19 and runs from 1:03:00 to 1:09:14 minutes on the DVD. (Queue up this scene before your session.)*

---

2. Guilt, various fears, failure, shame, and taking the easy way out were all dragging Simba down. In what ways can you relate to Simba?

3. What are some of the relational and personal issues that can weigh us down? In what ways do those weights affect the way we cope with life? Give an example.

4. In what ways did the discussion between Simba and his father remind you of Saul's story on the road to Damascus?

5. In the same way Simba's father reminded Simba of who he really was, your Father in heaven loves you and wants you to know that you're more than you've become. He longs to see you become all He created you to be. How does it make you feel, really?

Prayer is the most important thing we can do to work together on the journey. What are your hopes for this group? How can we pray for you today?

My Hopes & Prayer Requests:

My Group's Hopes & Prayer Requests:

Closing Recovery Prayer:

Lord, thanks for bringing each person that joined us today. We've made a start, so now together we join you on the path. We keep going because nothing else has worked, but we cannot make it alone. We invite You to join with us, and help us find our way. Help us remember that we're more than we've become.

Taking it Home

LEADER: *Explain that "Taking it Home" for each session contains a set of personal questions to take you deeper in your own story. In addition, there's either an introspective question to ask of your heart or a question to take to God. Emphasize that it's essential to the recovery process to complete these take-home activities. Be sure to highlight the importance of keeping a daily journal of thoughts, feelings, and key insights that God reveals. Journaling is a powerful tool*

MY STORY: Trust in the Spirit of God to open your eyes & heart as you write.

1. Do I have any apprehension, hesitancy, or fears about being involved in this recovery process? (List them here.) What specifically is making me uncomfortable?

2. What are some of the key things I'd like to have happen in my life as a result of being a part of this group?

NOTE: Be sure to review the Group Covenant in the next page so you're prepared for a brief group discussion at the next meeting.

A QUESTION TO TAKE TO MY HEART:

When you ask a question of your heart, don't analyze it intellectually; rather, look into your heart to find where your true attitudes and unexamined motives lurk. Grapple with what drives your behavior. Dig for what you really believe in the deep recesses of your heart about God, yourself, and the world in which you live. Be sure to capture the responses in writing

* My hang-ups and addictions are dragging me down, and yet I still keep turning back to them. What's driving that? When I'm honest with myself, what is it I'm really after?

IDEAS FOR YOUR DAILY JOURNAL: (as simple as a spiral notebook)
  - New things I'm learning and accepting in this process
  - Thoughts and feelings about myself, God, other people, and my life situation
  - Behaviors related to my addiction or compulsion
  - Failures I've had
  - Victories (even small steps in the right direction)

GROUP COVENANT

As you begin this study, it is important that your group covenant together, agreeing to live out important group values. Once these values are agreed upon, your group will be on its way to experiencing true redemptive community. It's very important that your group discuss these values—preferably as you begin this study.

* PRIORITY: While we are in this group, we will give the group meetings priority. All the sessions are integrated, with each session building on the sessions that precede them. Committed attendance is vital to overcoming your addictions.

  NOTE: Due to the focus of this group on taking the journey through grief and loss, group sessions will require a full 90 minutes to complete, so plan accordingly.

* PARTICIPATION AND FAIRNESS: Because we are here to receive help, we commit to participation and interaction in the group. No one dominates. We will be fair to others and concentrate on telling our own stories briefly.

* HOMEWORK: The homework experiences are an integral and vital part of the recovery process. The assignments between each session might include: (1) A Question to Take to My Heart; (2) A Question to Take to God; (3) Questions about your story; and (4) Activities that must be completed to continue on with your 12-Step Recovery Map.

* RESPECT AND OWNERSHIP: Everyone is given the right to his or her own opinions, and all questions are encouraged and respected. We will not judge or condemn as others share their stories. We are each responsible for our own recovery and will not "own" someone else's. Offensive language is not permitted.

* CONFIDENTIALITY: Anything that is said in our meetings is never repeated outside the meeting without permission for all of your group members. This is vital in creating the environment of trust and openness required to facilitate the healing and freedom. The persons attending this group will be known only to one another. Names of attendees will not be shared with others.

* LIFE CHANGE: We will regularly assess our progress and will complete the "Taking it Home" activities to reinforce what we are learning and better integrate those lessons into our personal journeys.

* CARE AND SUPPORT: Permission is given to call upon each other at any time, especially in times of crisis. The group will provide care for every member.

* ACCOUNTABILITY AND INTEGRITY: We agree to let the members of our group hold us accountable to commitments we make in whatever loving ways we decide upon. Unsolicited advice giving is not permitted. We will seek out and build a close relationship with an accountability partner for mutual growth and responsibility. Men will help to men and women will help to women in order to uphold the spirit of integrity.

* EXPECTATIONS OF FACILITATORS: This meeting is not professional therapy. We are not licensed therapists. Group facilitators are volunteers whose only desire is to encourage people in finding freedom and hope.

I agree to all of the above_____ Date: _____

WE CAN'T DO IT ON OUR OWN (STEP 1)

BREAKING THE ICE - 15 MINUTES

> **LEADER:** *Encourage each group member to give a response to the "Breaking the Ice" questions. This gets people joining in on lighter topics. If someone can't think of an answer say, "We'll come back to you." After others in the room have shared, swing back around to people you skipped.*

1. As child, which of the following superheroes did you pretend to be and why?
   - ☐ Superman or Clark Kent? – I'm not really sure who I am, but I like saving the world.
   - ☐ X-men – I like to work as part of a team.
   - ☐ Wonder Woman – I'm deflecting all the enemies bullets and lassoing evil.
   - ☐ The Lone Ranger – I can make it on my own ... hi ho Silver, away ...
   - ☐ Batman – I come out from my cave from time to time and surprise people.
   - ☐ Spider-Man – I hang out, often feeling misunderstood and confused.
   - ☐ Other: _____

2. Was there ever a time you tried to be a "superhero" and rescue someone in real life and the whole deal blew up in your face? Briefly share your story.

3. How did your "Taking it Home" assignment go? Did you spend some time alone? Would you share one key insight from the time in your story?

Opening Prayer:

Holy Spirit, please join us in our session today. We want to see things as they really are. We tried so hard to break free from the stuff that's controlling our lives, but we keep getting dragged back in. Help us to be honest with ourselves, with each other, and with You. Strengthen each of us as we begin to understand the reality of our addictions.

In our introductory session: We learned that we don't have to go it alone. We uncovered several core values and 12 steps needed in our journey to recovery and freedom. As we looked at the life of Saul, we saw an obsessed man driving his life in a dangerous direction who was transformed by personal encounters with Jesus. We like Saul are "more than we've become" and through this journey together we can find real change.

In Step 1: We'd never actually say, "I'm God, I can handle anything that comes my way." Yet, we've spent most of our lives believing we could do life just fine on our own. It's a nice theory, but we're all here because we've figured out it doesn't really work. We've tried and tried to shake the grip of whatever is making our lives unmanageable ... and we just can't.

Objectives for this step:
- Become aware of the danger of isolation – going it alone
- Identify signs and discover statements that highlight areas of denial
- Admit life is unmanageable and we're powerless over our addictions and compulsions
- Focus on who we are by separating our identity from our addictions

Discovering the Truth - 30 minutes

> **LEADER:** *Read the questions and explanations to the group. Encourage everyone to participate and allow people to discover truth through group discussions, but keep things moving. Ask for volunteers to read Bible passages. Be sure to leave time for "Embracing the Truth" and "Connecting."*

1. What's your gut-level response when you hear easy answer clichés like "Just say no" or "Give it all to Jesus"?

We all experience pain in our lives and there are many ways to "numb out." Trying to escape our pain or seek pleasure in a tough world are the reasons we get trapped in addictions. Have you ever wondered how God feels about the pain in your life and mine?

They dress the wound of my people as though it is not serious. "Peace, peace," they say, when there is not peace.

JEREMIAH 6:14 NIV

2. God is clearly critical of religious leaders here. What attitudes toward people's pain and struggles is God criticizing? (Reread the verse.) When God looks at the messes in our our lives, what does He zero in on? How does He feel about us and our addictions?

Let's launch into Step 1 of our Recovery Map : ADMIT YOUR NEED: We admit that life has become unmanageable, and that we're powerless over our addictions, compulsive behavior, and life direction.

RECOVERY MAP

STARTING WITH DECISION	**1. Admit your need**
	2. Find new power
	3. Make a decision
SEARCHING MY SELF	4. Take inventory
	5. Admit your addiction to others
	6. Prepare for change
SEEKING HEALING & CHANGE	7. Ask God to restore & redeem life
	8. Identify resentments & offenses
	9. Make amends
STICKING WITH IT	10. Be preventative
	11. Stay connected with God
	12. Share your story

Taken Captive

We all want to be free—to really enjoy life. None of us likes dealing with the pain and hurts in our lives. Our desire to find meaning, significance, belonging, adventure, and close relationships send us searching. So, how did we end up trapped and powerless over our addictions?

[16] Do you not know that if you offer yourselves to someone as obedient slaves, you are slaves to that one you obey—either of sin leading to death or obedience [following God] leading to righteousness? [17] But thank God that, although you used to be slaves of sin, you obeyed from the heart that pattern of teaching you were entrusted to, [18] and having been liberated from sin, you became enslaved to righteousness.

ROMANS 6:16-18 HCSB

It was for freedom that Christ set us free; therefore keep standing firm and do not be subject again to the yoke of slavery.

GALATIANS 5:1 NASB

God knows how we're wired inside and out, and He's not just concerned about our behaviors, but what drives them on the inside (in our heart, mind, and spirit). He designed us to be free and experience a full and meaningful life.

3. What are the two masters identified in Romans 6:16 and Jeremiah 2:13? What do these verses, along with Galatians 5:1, say will happen if we live out of our old well-worn patterns and ruts, rather than taking our deepest needs, desires, and thirsts to God?

We all have our "drug of choice" when life gets tough: spending, drinking, drugs, doughnuts, overworking, porn, TV, or whatever it is. Sooner or later, these things can control us and we become enslaved and powerless to someone or something. Listen to the Apostle Paul as he describes the battle going on inside each one of us ...

[18] I know that nothing good lives in me, that is, in my flesh. For the desire to do what is good is with me, but there is no ability to do it. [19] For I do not do the good that I want to do, but I practice the evil that I do not want to do. [20] Now if I do what I do not want, I am no longer the one doing it, but it is the sin that lives in me.

ROMANS 7:18-20 HCSB

4. How would you describe the inner struggle that Paul is explaining in Romans 7:18-20? In what ways can you relate?

POWERLESS

Paul is very aware of what's going on inside himself and inside all of us. He pulls no punches and sugarcoats nothing.

²¹ ... when I want to do good, evil is with me. ²² For in my inner self I joyfully agree with God's law. ²³ But I see a different law in the parts of my body, waging war against the law of my mind and taking me prisoner to the law of sin in the parts of my body. ²⁴ What a wretched man I am! Who will rescue me from this body of death? ROMANS 7:21-24 HCSB

5. Even a great man like the Apostle Paul really struggled ... he was human. What emotions do you think Paul was feeling in verses 21-24? What did Paul realize about himself and the power he had over the assaults to his mind and heart?

6. After Paul admits he's powerless, what does he look for (verse 24)? Does this make him weak? Explain.

7. In general, how do you feel about the prospect of being powerless? When you feel powerless, how do you tend to respond?

Truth is, we're all powerless to change ourselves—our humanness and our old nature. Many children dream of flying like Superman or Peter Pan, but no matter how hard we try we all resign ourselves to flying in a plane. We can't change our spiritual condition or our hearts any more than we can make ourselves fly. Like Paul, we need a rescuer.

The only power we've each been given by God is the power to choose—to decide what we will believe and what we won't, whether we'll try to run our own life or turn to the only One who can rescue us. That's what the first three steps of our Recovery Map are about ... starting with DECISION.

Embracing the Truth - 20 minutes

Decision Roadblocks

Step 1 is vital to moving forward toward healing and recovery. Unless we're honest with ourselves and see ourselves as we really are (as the Apostle Paul did), we'll stay stuck or continue to spiral down. There are two major roadblocks.

Roadblock 1: Denial

The trouble with denial is that we often don't even know we're doing it. We've bought into lies for so long, we really believe them. We've believed that our habits, behaviors, and addictions aren't really all that bad. We've rationalized and made excuses until we believe our own rationalizations.

1. What are some things we watch for to tell that someone we know is living in denial—not accepting the reality of things? How can we identify denial in our own lives?

Here are a few symptoms that suggest a person might be living in denial:

Defensiveness: "I become angry and fight back when people try to point out a weakness." If people are able to admit their need and are open to growing, they're less likely to become defensive to constructive criticism and opinions.

Argumentative: "I make excuses or refuse to consider people's observations." If we want to find freedom, it's time to speak the truth about addictions and behaviors.

Settling: "But ... I'm doing better than I used to." Our version "doing better" probably still has us living in bondage and dysfunction!

Covering up/Secrecy: "I hide my behavior and lie to cover it up." We tend to hide our problems. Healing & freedom come as we drop the veil of secrecy.

Preachyness: "I constantly tell others what their problems are and how to fix them." We're focusing on others to avoid taking a long, hard look at our own problems.

Rebellion: "No one is going to run my life or tell me what to do."
Either the dragon of rebellion raises its ugly head, or we build a thick brick wall around ourselves. It can be a rage over having been controlled or manipulated. For others it's because they feel they've not gotten their way in life; their goals have been thwarted.

2. When confronted with your addiction or destructive behavior, which of the signs of denial do you tend to display?

When pride comes, disgrace follows, but with humility comes wisdom. — PROVERBS 11:2 HCSB

3. What can we learn from this proverb about our attitude as we deal with our addictions and the unmanageable life they've created?

Roadblock 2: Buying into Lies

A primary goal in the recovery process is to recognize the lies you've accepted as truths and begin to speak the truth to yourself. Lies about yourself, God, other people, and the world in which we live, will keep you trapped in your harmful lifestyle.

One of lies is that you're the "bad guy," but the true villain in the story is working overtime to mess up your life. Jesus knows the enemy and his evil intent well.

[Jesus talking about the fallen angel who rules the demons ...] He was a murderer from the beginning and has not stood in the truth, because there is no truth in him. When he tells a lie, he speaks from his own nature, because he is a liar and the father of liars.

JOHN 8:44 HCSB

4. What is Jesus' attitude toward the villain in the larger story and in our own personal stories? How does Jesus describe his nature, intentions, and strategies in John 8;44?

The enemy's goal is to isolate you and take you out. He is the master deceiver. His strategy is to repeat lies over and over to get you to doubt the heart of God and your own value and dignity. If you believe the lies, you'll think, feel and act as if they were true.

We often agree with such lies as:
   "I should be able to do this on my own."
   "I'm a failure, so I can't stick with the program. This will never work."
   "If I can keep this a secret, no one will know or be hurt by my addiction."
   "I'm so far gone, I may as well give up."
   "I'd never be in this mess if it wasn't for _____."
   "How can I trust God after He gave me such a screwed up life? Why me?!"
   Other: _____

5. Are there any lies you hear over and over in your head that are holding you back from admitting your need and from following the Recovery Map?

Let's try speaking some truth together in unison (even if you not sure you believe it yet): "I have an enemy who has messed up my life and is trying to take me out. Even though I'm powerless to change things, God has the power. He loves me—the real me. He separates who I am from the addictions I'm trapped in, and He knows I'm really more than I've become."

CONNECTING - 25 MINUTES

LEADER: *Use this "Connecting" time to develop more closeness in the group. They will need each other's support and encouragement in very practical ways as they take this journey together. Set the model for openness and trust by being the first one to share part of your story with the group. Encourage everyone to participate, but remember that some won't be as comfortable opening up yet.*

LEADER INSTRUCTIONS FOR GROUP EXPERIENCE:
SUPPLIES: *A big green blob -- children's modeling clay or putty.*
EXPLAIN: *Hold the green blob in your hand as you reintroduce the topic of powerlessness. Explain that the blob represents the addiction we've been carrying around. The addiction is not who we are; it's not what defines us. It's a "thing" that's attached itself to us, and it's pulling us down.*
PROCEDURE: *You're going to pass the green blob around to each person in the group—you go first—and ask each person to share a few things about the "rock" they've been dragging around.*

In our first session, we talked about trying to run a race when we're weighted down? Let's have this green blob represent the addictions and the habits that are keeping us from running successfully. Let's get the thing out of our hearts and look at it, talk about it. Just like the blob is an "it," our addictions are things that have attached themselves to us, and trapped us. They don't define us; they are not us; we're not the sum of our addictions.

Starting with the leader, each of you will take the blob, and share your thoughts on questions 1-4 with the group. After your turn, pass the rock to the next person.

1. We have kept our "blob" inside, hidden it as a secret part of us, hoping no one would ever discover it. What are some things you've done to cover up your addictive behaviors?

2. How do think secrecy might actually increase the power of the "blob" in our lives?

3. Whose lives do you believe are being most affected by the consequences of your struggle with your behaviors and "drug of choice"? What do you think will happen to them if you continue in your addiction?

4. Identify where you are in this first step of the journey: Defining your "blob" and admitting you are powerless over your addiction and compulsive behavior.

1	2	3	4	5	6	7	8	9	10
I don't know what my blob is			I can define my blob & I'm trying to remove it!				Help! I can't stop it on my own		

Go ahead and demonstrate to the blob how you really feel about it right now.

How can we pray for you today?

MY PRAYER REQUESTS:

MY GROUP'S PRAYER REQUESTS:

CLOSING RECOVERY PRAYER:

God, we won't pretend. It's not easy to admit we have a problem, and it's even tougher to admit we're powerless to really do anything about it. Give us courage this week to face the truth. Thanks for this group. Help us together to commit to staying with this journey no matter how difficult is becomes.

GROUP COVENANT REVIEW:

Take time as a group to review and sign the Group Covenant on page 19. Make any adjustments that the majority of the group members, and the group leader, can support.

TAKING IT HOME

> **LEADER:** *Remind your group that "Taking it Home" contains personal questions to take us deeper in our own stories. This week, there's a question to ask their heart. Emphasize again that it's essential to the recovery process to complete these take-home activities. Keep reinforcing the importance of keeping a daily journal of thoughts, feelings, and key insights God reveals. Journaling is a powerful tool. You should also encourage people to begin thinking about an accountability partner (see page 8).*

My Story: Trust in the Holy Spirit to open your eyes & heart as you write.

1. What habit patterns and destructive behaviors are causing my life to be unmanageable? How intense is the difficulty and pain from these things?

2. What have I tried to overcome my destructive behaviors or to get life back under control? How have these things worked for me?

3. What if I don't change ... where will I be 5 years from now? If I allow the blob to stay and grow, where will it take me in the future? How will affect other people in my life?

A Question to Take to My Heart:

This is a time for introspection and reflection. It's a time to grapple with what drives your thinking and behavior—what you believe in the deep recesses of your heart about God, yourself, and the world in which you live. Be sure to write down your responses.

> ✳ To what degree have I attached my self image to my addiction? What lies have I been believing about myself? About my behaviors and addiction?

Ideas for Your Daily Journal: (as simple as a spiral notebook)
- New things I'm learning and accepting in this process
- Thoughts and feelings about myself, God, other people, and my life situation
- Behaviors related to my addiction or compulsion ... and people who are getting hurt
- Lies I've been believing & excuses I've been making
- Failures and ... Victories (even small steps in the right direction)

I'm fully ready to take Step 1: I admit that my life has become unmanageable, and that I'm powerless over my addictions, compulsive behavior, and life direction.

Signed _____ Date: _____

Hope to Stop the Madness (Step 2)

Breaking the Ice - 15 minutes

> **LEADER:** *The goal of the "Breaking the Ice" questions is to help put people at ease and encourage group members to get better acquainted as they begin talking casually about the session topic. Keep the tone of the conversation light and be sure everyone gets a turn.*

1. Complete the following sentence: "The most insane or nutty thing I ever heard about or saw somebody do was ..."

2. Which of the following reality TV shows best describes how you feel when someone is driving the car and you end up in the passenger seat (or worse, the back seat)? Explain.
   - ☐ *Survivor* – It's all about how you control the game; I've gotta get that wheel back!
   - ☐ *The Great American Race* – Put the pedal to the metal baby & let's roll!
   - ☐ *Trading Spaces* – Anything could happen, but we'll give it a shot.
   - ☐ *What Not to Wear* – With the way I look *and* drive, it's best to let anybody else steer.
   - ☐ *Three Wishes* – (1) Make me king. (2) Give me a limo. (3) I pick my own driver.
   - ☐ Other: _____

3. How did your "Taking it Home" assignment go? As you spent time in your story, what did you learn about your current path, or any lies you believed about your addiction?

> **LEADER:** *Explain to group members that the 12 Steps build on each other, and that it's important not to gloss over any steps. Be sure they understand that each person will progress through the 12 Steps at HIS OR HER OWN PACE. Encourage people to stay real and honest with themselves as they continue to wrestle with the step they are on.*

4. We never want to pretend or push people through steps they're still wrestling with, but did any of you sign Step 1 as completed? If you did, would you like to share with the group how you feel about that? If not, would you like to share something you're wrestling with?

OPENING PRAYER:

God, we want to step out of the insanity of our behavior and gain a new outlook. Please open our eyes so we can see how our lives are affected by forces inside of us and outside. Help this group to continue growing into a supportive, Redemptive Community.

IN STEP 1: We admitted our lives had become unmanageable. We embraced our powerlessness. Lie-based thinking has clouded our decision making, so we discussed our inner struggles, and identified key roadblocks to making constructive decisions about our lives. Finally, we also recognized that we can't go it alone, and determined not to isolate.

IN STEP 2: We'll focus on embracing the truth that it requires a Power greater than ourselves to restore us to sanity—to change us and set us free. To do this we need to understand the forces at work in our lives, and embrace God's power that can overcome them.

OBJECTIVES FOR THIS STEP:

- Recognize the insanity of our addictions
- Unveil the forces at work in our lives, choices, and behaviors
- Understand the motivators for our choices, behaviors, and addictions
- Begin to assess our feelings about our situation
- Embrace our need for a new source of power—a Power greater than ourselves

DISCOVERING THE TRUTH - 35 MINUTES

Let's press on into Step 2 of our Recovery Map: FIND NEW POWER: We embrace the truth that it requires a Power greater than ourselves to restore us to sanity, and to set us free.

RECOVERY MAP

STARTING WITH	1	1. Admit your need
DECISION	**2**	**2. Find new power**
	3	3. Make a decision
SEARCHING	4	4. Take inventory
MY SELF	5	5. Admit your addiction to others
	6	6. Prepare for change
SEEKING HEALING	7	7. Ask God to restore & redeem life
& CHANGE	8	8. Identify resentments & offenses
	9	9. Make amends
STICKING	10	10. Be preventative
WITH IT	11	11. Stay connected with God
	12	12. Share your story

LEADER: *After discussing the insanity of addictions and the forces and motivators behind them, you'll transition into reconnecting with the source of real power. Read the questions and explanations to the group. Model openness as you share, encourage everyone to participate, and allow discovery to happen. Keep things moving, and be sure to leave time for "Embracing the Truth" and "Connecting."*

THIS IS NUTS!

Last time we pulled out the green blob to represent our addiction, the thing that holds us captive. As we expose our blob for what it is, we'll soon realize that it causes insanity.

INSANITY could be defined as "repeating the same self-gratifying, destructive behaviors over and over again while expecting different results." A story is told about country music star Willie Nelson coming home drunk again, apparently expecting his wife at the time not to notice or to welcome the king of the castle home with open arms. She made him sleep it off in the living room again, but this time she sewed his sheets tightly together all the way around his body. When she was done, she grabbed a broom and beat him soundly with it and went to bed. The result: Willie is still getting drunk ... now that's insanity! Addictions are not a modern problem. Listen to these warnings from the 10th century B.C. to King Solomon's sons:

³ Do not crave his [a rich man's] delicacies, for that food is deceptive ... ²⁷ A prostitute is a deep pit and a wayward wife is a narrow well ... ³² [speaking of alcohol] In the end it bites like a snake and poisons like a viper. ³³ Your eyes will see strange sights and your mind imagine confusing things ... ³⁵ "They hit me," you will say, "but I'm not hurt! They beat me, but I don't feel it! When will I wake up so I can find another drink."

PROVERBS 23:3,27, 32-33, 35 NIV

1. What insane activities do you see in the three different cravings or addictions warned about in this proverb?

2. What are some insane behaviors you've found yourself doing?
   - ☐ Continuing to do things that hurt others I care about or myself
   - ☐ Doing things, thinking there will be no consequences or "it won't happen to me"
   - ☐ Believing that I really can have it all ... everything that I want
   - ☐ Blaming others for my behaviors or making up lame excuses
   - ☐ Cutting myself off from the lifelines that could pull me out
   - ☐ Trying to beat this thing my own way ... again and again
   - ☐ Getting almost over the problem, then sabotaging it all
   - ☐ Other: _____

FORCES THAT PULL US TOWARD INSANITY

¹ And you were dead in your trespasses and sins, ² in which you formerly walked according to the course of this world, according to the prince of the power of the air, of the spirit that is now working in the sons of disobedience. ³ Among them we too all formerly lived in the lusts of our flesh, indulging the desires of the flesh and of the mind, and were by nature children of wrath, even as the rest.

EPHESIANS 2:1-3 NASB

3. What are the three distinct influences identified in verses 2 and 3 that pull us down into actions that are damaging to ourselves and others? What's likely to happen if we aren't alert to all three forces?

Do not conform any longer to the pattern of this world, but be transformed by the renewing of your mind. Then you will be able to test and approve what God's will is — His good, pleasing, and perfect will.

ROMANS 12:2 NIV

4. In the battle that rages for our hearts, what do you believe is the strong draw of the world patterns and values mentioned in Romans 12:2 Ephesians 2:2?

The heart is more deceitful than anything else and desperately sick—who can understand it?

JEREMIAH 17:9 HCSB

5. According to Jeremiah 17:9, what was our old heart like before we trusted Jesus for life?

[18] I know that nothing good lives in me, that is, in my flesh. For the desire to do what is good is with me, but there is no ability to do it. [19] For I do not do the good that I want to do, but I practice the evil that I do not want to do. [20] Now if I do what I do not want, I am no longer the one doing it, but it is the sin that lives in me. ROMANS 7:18-20 HCSB

6. Did sin just go away when we became Christians? What does Romans 7:20 identify as the culprit for our sin after we've been re-created in Christ (1 Corinthians 5:17) and given a new regenerated heart (Ezekiel 36:26-27)?

Before we know Jesus personally, our poor choices come from a deceitful, depraved heart. Once, we become re-created through Jesus, our poor choices come from the old established patterns of thinking and behavior, which keep us from living out of our new heart. In the final analysis, we own our choices. We're also affected by the world's values and the evil in the world around us. But the third force is the real villain in the story.

[11] Put on the full armor of God so that you can stand against the tactics of the Devil. [12] For our battle is not against flesh and blood, but against the rulers, against the authorities, against the world powers of this darkness, against the spiritual forces of evil in the heavens.

EPHESIANS 6:11-12 HCSB

Be of sober spirit, be on the alert. Your adversary, the devil, prowls around like a roaring lion seeking someone to devour. 1 PETER 3:8 NASB

7. In Ephesians 6:11-12 and 1 Peter 3:8, who is identified as the "prince of the power of the air" (Ephesians 2:2), the "rulers of this darkness"? What is his intent for you and me?

FIGHTING FOR OUR LIVES

We've seen that the enemy forces that are trying to take us out are (1) our distorted desires and well-worn patterns of behavior; (2) a world system that's under the control of Satan himself; and (3) very real and active spiritual forces we can't even see. In military terms, conventional weapons aren't going to save us.

⁴ The weapons we fight with are not the weapons of the world. On the contrary , they have divine power to demolish strongholds. ⁵ We demolish arguments and every pretension that sets itself up against the knowledge of God and we take every thought captive.

2 CORINTHIANS 10:4-5 NIV

8. What's the source of the weapons the Apostle Paul is talking about in 2 Corinthians 10:4? Why do these weapons "demolish" the forces that we are powerless over?

9. Why do you think the focus is on our thoughts and beliefs as the real battlefield in verse 5, as opposed to our behavior or our feelings?

EMBRACING THE TRUTH - 20 MINUTES

The enemy's favorite tactic is deception. Lie-based thinking is at the root of most of our destructive behavior because every behavior has an underlying belief. He strategically tries to deceive us to (1) question God's goodness, (2) doubt the heart of God toward us, (3) believe we have the power in and of ourselves to stop the insanity, and (4) turn to imposters—people, things, careers, activities, anything that takes the place of God.

[God speaking in metaphor:] "For My people have committed a double evil: They have abandoned Me, the fountain of living water, and dug cisterns for themselves, cracked cisterns that cannot hold water."

JEREMIAH 2:13 HCSB

1. What do the cisterns in Jeremiah 2:13 represent? What happens when we fall into relying on our own resources rather than taking our deepest thirsts to God?

2. Why do you think that we so easily abandon God, and turn to counterfeit lovers?

Sin is still present in us. We swing between self-gratification and self-pity, from trying to control life to protect ourselves and hiding in shame and failure. In Session 1, we learned that the very things we turn to in order to escape pain and feel good only work for a short time – they're nothing more than sedatives that keep us numb. These sedatives keep us coming back for more, and draw our hearts from the Power that can break the cycle and restore our sanity.

3. Which of the following false beliefs do you feel vulnerable to? Please explain.
   ☐ Questioning the goodness or power of God
   ☐ Doubting the heart of God toward me personally
   ☐ Believing I have the power in and of myself to stop the insanity, and end up trapped by God-imposters
   ☐ Turning my heart to counterfeit lovers (people, activities, careers, stuff, substances, food, etc.)
   ☐ Other: _____

In 2 Corinthians 10:4-5, we learned that we need weapons with "divine power"—a Power greater than ourselves to "demolish strongholds" in our lives. Our enemy doesn't want us to find these weapons, this new Power. Let's consider the truth about God's heart toward us that He Himself reveals to us ...

[12] The Father ... has enabled you to share in the saints' inheritance in the light. [13] He has rescued us from the domain of darkness and transferred us into the kingdom of the Son He loves, [14] in whom we have redemption, the forgiveness of sins.

COLOSSIANS 1:12-14 HCSB

[11] "I know the plans I have for you," declares the LORD, "plans to prosper you and not to harm you, plans to give you hope and a future. [12] Then you will call upon me and come and pray to me, and I will listen to you. [13] You will seek me and find me when you seek me with your whole heart. [14] I will be found by you," declares the LORD, "and will bring you back from captivity."

JEREMIAH 29:11-14 NIV

3. What do Colossians 1 and Jeremiah 29 show us about the heart of God toward us? What promises from God do we find in these two passages?

4. The Bible makes it clear that we have to fight for our freedom. What does that require from us according to Jeremiah 29:12-13?

CONNECTING - 20 MINUTES

LEADER: *Use this "Connecting" time to develop a sense of community, that we're all in this together. Remind the group that we're wrestling with deep issues of the heart that don't have a quick Band-Aid® fix. Encourage people to be real and jump into the fight. Invite people of the same gender to contact each other during the week. It's time for them to support each other in the battle.*

We must embrace the belief that we can lead a life of freedom and abundance. It is possible! It's this belief that brings a sense of hope. When we truly believe that God can do what we can't, we are ready for His power to begin to flow through our lives. The first step toward sanity is faith. There is a deciding moment of belief when we turn the corner and accept the fact that only God could create peace in the midst of our chaos.
Our behavior is the best indicator of our truest, deepest beliefs, not our intellectual stance. It's what we really believe in our heart of hearts that will drive our recovery. Let's try some "listening prayer" to help us begin to get a handle on what we truly believe ...

LISTENING PRAYER TIME:

You're going to lead group members in a short time of listening prayer.
- *Allow this experience some time; don't rush it.*
- *Put on quiet background music (use the CD Pursued by God: Redemptive Worship Volume 1 from Serendipity House, or select your own music); dim the lights if possible.*
- *Help each person create a small personal area. This is not a time to chat; make it very honoring.*
- *Trust God to speak to each person individually.*

1.   When you were visualizing your addiction, what did it look like?

2. Was God there at the chasm with you? Where? How does He feel about your struggles?

The Spirit of the Sovereign LORD *is upon me to preach good news to the poor. He sent me to bind up the brokenhearted, to proclaim freedom for the captives and release from darkness for the prisoners, to proclaim the year of the* LORD*'s favor and the day of vengeance of our God, to comfort all who mourn, to provide for those who grieve in Zion—to bestow on them the crown of beauty instead of ashes, the oil of gladness instead of mourning, and a garment of praise instead of a spirit of despair.*
ISAIAH 61:1-3 HCSB

3. What hope and promise did you hear in these words? Was there a particular word or phrase that gave you a sense of hope or anticipation?

Is there any way that this group can support you practically in specific ways this week as you confront the insanity of your life? How can we pray for you today? Each person should pray for the person to his or her right.

MY PRAYER REQUESTS & NEEDS:

MY GROUP'S PRAYER REQUESTS & NEEDS:

CLOSING RECOVERY PRAYER:

Jesus, we are so thankful that Your passion and mission is to bind up the brokenhearted, set captives free and replace beauty for ashes in our lives! Help us this week to embrace Your divinely powerful weapons and demolish the destructive "self-talk" we hear playing over and over in our minds.

TAKING IT HOME

LEADER: *Strongly encourage everyone to spend time taking the truths learned today into their own stories by answering the questions and keeping a daily journal of memories, thoughts, actions, feelings, struggles, and key insights that God reveals. These will greatly enhance both individual and group experiences in the recovery process.*

It's just a bunch of nice sounding words and hot air if we don't take this stuff home with us. Go ahead, fight through your doubts and fears with God. He's a big God and He can take it. Stay with the 12 Steps and expect some victories this week!

QUESTIONS TO TAKE TO MY HEART:

Search deep into your heart to answer the following questions. This is a time for introspection and reflection; it's a time to grapple with what really drives your thinking and behavior. What you really believe in your innermost self, not what you say you believe, is what becomes central to your personal recovery.

✳ How am I being influenced? What am I aware of regarding (1) old sin patterns, (2) the world's answers, and (3) the enemy's subtle assaults?

✳ What do my destructive behaviors tell me that I really believe, deep down inside, about God, myself, my relationships, and the world in which I live?

IDEAS FOR YOUR DAILY JOURNAL: (as simple as a spiral notebook)

- Insane things I find myself doing
- Attacks from the enemy, my old nature, and the world on my recovery
- Thoughts and feelings about myself, God, other people, and my life situation
- Lies I've been believing & the truths replacing them
- Failures and temporary setbacks
- Victories (even small steps in the right direction)

Do I want things to change enough that I'm willing to risk trusting God and releasing my grip on the controls of my life?

I still have some questions, but I'm fully ready to take Step 2: I embrace the truth that it requires a Power greater than myself to restore me to sanity—to set me free.

Signed_____ Date:_____

THE POWER TO CHOOSE ... USE IT! (STEP 3)

BREAKING THE ICE - 15 MINUTES

1. Unsolved Mysteries: If you could solve a historical mystery, which of the following would it be? Explain why this mystery appeals to you.
   - ☐ Was there truly an Atlantis civilization?
   - ☐ What are the pyramids really about? Were they landing strips for aliens?
   - ☐ Why is it a woman's prerogative to change her mind?
   - ☐ Is there life on other planets?
   - ☐ Why do I pay more taxes than Donald Trump?
   - ☐ Other: _____

2. We all have unknown parts to our story, mysteries. Share a secret talent, interest, experience, or "hidden gem" from your life that might be interesting to the group.

3. What's one mystery about God that baffles you the most?

4. How did your "Taking it Home" assignment go this week? What did you discover about the influencers in your life, and any true beliefs that affect your behavior?

OPENING PRAYER:

God, many of us are seeing new glimpses of reality that we never considered before. Our thinking is being stretched, and some of the openness and accountability in this group makes us squirm a little. We know though, that at the end of each day, each one of us sets our paths by the decisions we make. Join us and speak to our hearts as we talk about a pivotal decision in our recovery.

IN STEP 2: We embraced the truth that it requires a Power greater than ourselves to restore us to sanity—to change us and set us free. To do this we unveiled the forces at work in our lives (the world, our distorted passions, and our enemy). Then we began to explore the heart of God toward us and the divinely powerful weapons He offers.

IN STEP 3: Our choices about what to believe and do are vital to healing and freedom.

OBJECTIVES FOR THIS STEP:

- Uncover the mystery and the power in our free will
- Recognize the tension between distorted desires and the new heart God gives us
- Understand the pull between old habit patterns and the "new creation" God makes us
- Begin to see the real heart of God
- Grasp the importance of turning our hearts to God and allowing Him to write our story of healing, freedom, and wholeness

DISCOVERING THE TRUTH - 35 MINUTES

LEADER: *Ask for volunteers to read the passages. You should read the questions and explana-tions to the group. Become very familiar with the Bible passages and be prepared to answer any questions or objections. Be sure to leave time for "Embracing the Truth" and "Connecting" segment.*

Today we approach the closing step in "Starting with Decision" from our Recovery Map: MAKE A DECISION: We make a decision to chose life, and TO turn our lives and our wills over to the care of God more and more as we know Him deeper.

Recovery Map

STARTING WITH	I	1. Admit your need
DECISION	2	2. Find new power
	3	**3. Make a decision**
SEARCHING	4	4. Take inventory
MY SELF	5	5. Admit your addiction to others
	6	6. Prepare for change
SEEKING HEALING	7	7. Ask God to restore & redeem life
& CHANGE	8	8. Identify resentments & offenses
	9	9. Make amends
STICKING	10	10. Be preventative
WITH IT	11	11. Stay connected with God
	12	12. Share your story

We've discovered only God has the power to set us free from the beliefs and addictions that hold us hostage. To access His power we must seek God with our "whole heart."

THE MYSTERY OF FREE WILL

God created us in His image (Genesis 1:27) with the freedom to choose. Ever since Adam's and Eve's choice to distrust and turn away from loving God in the Garden of Eden, the world has been anything but the perfect paradise God created.

1. Why would God take the risk of creating human beings with free will, after being betrayed the first time he'd done this? (Lucifer, with a third of the angels, had staged a massive rebellion in heaven and been cast out - Isaiah 14:12-15.)

The answer is that without this risk and freedom, there can be no real relationship. We were created to be in relationship, both with our Creator and with other people. We were made for the ecstasy that relationships can bring, including worship of God, the oneness of marriage (for many), and the intimacy of close friendships and family.

As a result of the deception of man by Satan in the Garden of Eden, and the subsequent fall of man into sin and rebellion, our desires and passions became distorted. So, we end up giving our hearts and lives to empty imposters and counterfeit lovers that can never satisfy us. Ezekiel refers to counterfeit lovers that take God's place as "idols" in our heart.

⁴This is what the Sovereign LORD says: When any Israelite sets up idols in his heart he puts a wicked stumbling block before his face ... I the LORD will answer him myself in keeping with his great idolatry. ⁵ I will do this to recapture the hearts of the people ... ⁶ Turn from your idols and all your detestable practices ... ¹¹ The the people of Israel will no longer stray from me, nor will they defile themselves anymore with all their sins. They will be my people and I will be their God.

EZEKIEL 14:4-6,11 NIV

2. As you read God's words in Ezekiel 14, what emotions come through? What is God feeling about the counterfeit lovers in our hearts?

3. What are God's two motivations for pleading with us to turn from the counterfeits that master us, and then turn to Him with our deepest desires (verses 5 and 11)?

The Apostle Paul also refers to our distorted desires and the solution to correct them:

²² Put off your old self, which is being corrupted by its deceitful desires; ²³ ... be made new in the attitude of your minds; ²⁴ ... put on the new self, created to be like God in true righteousness and holiness.

EPHESIANS 4:22-24 NIV

4. According to Ephesians 4:22-24 why should we put off the old self and put on the new self? Where does this "new self" come from?

Oh, that their hearts would be inclined to fear me and keep all my commands always, so that it might go well with them and their children forever!

DEUTERONOMY 5:29 NIV

5. Why is God pleading in Deuteronomy 5:29 to His people? Why should we turn to Him for care and direction?

I'M A MESS ... HOW CAN I BE CONNECTED WITH GOD?

We all carry some haunting questions around about God. Sure, He's God so He has to be loving and merciful. But the questions we want answered are: "Does God love ME?" and "Will God accept ME with all my baggage and the mess I've made of my life?" Jesus told this story to give us a clear picture of the heart of God and how to please our Father.

[11] *There was a man who had two sons.* [12] *The younger one said to his father, 'Father, give me my share of the estate.' So he divided his property between them.* [13] *Not long after that, the younger son got together all he had, set off for a distant country and there squandered his wealth in wild living.*

[14] *After he spent everything, there was a severe famine in that whole country, and he began to be in need.* [15] *So he sent and hired himself out to a citizen of that country, who sent him to his fields to feed pigs.* [16] *He longed to fill his stomach with the pods that the pigs were eating, but no one gave him anything.*

6. The son in the story was a man whose desires got distorted. His heart turned from his father to counterfeit lovers, and destructive choices followed. What were some of his distorted desires and lifeless objects of his affections? Name one God-given desire in *your* life that has been distorted, and one of *your* substitutes for God.

[17] *When he came to his senses, he said, 'How many of my father's hired men have food to spare, and here I am starving to death!* [18] *I will set out and go back to my father and say to him, Father, I have sinned against heaven and against you.* [19] *I am no longer worthy to be called your son; make me like one of your hired men.'*

[20] *So he got up and went to his father. But while he was still a long way off, his father saw him and was filled with compassion for him; he ran to his son, threw his arms around him, and kissed him.* [21] *The son said to him, 'Father, I have sinned against heaven and against you. I am no longer worthy to be called your son.'*

²² "But the father told his servants, 'Quick! Bring the best robe and put it on him. Put a ring on his finger and sandals on his feet. ²³ Bring the fattened calf and kill it. Let's have a feast and celebrate. ²⁴ For this son of mine was dead and is alive again; he was lost and is found.' So they began to celebrate.

LUKE 15:11-24 NIV

7. Just like the son is this story, we all reach a point where our choices give us a wake-up call. Have you had a wake-up call? What got your attention about your addiction?

8. This son came to his senses, admitted his need, and embraced the truth that he needed a power greater than himself. Describe the internal dynamic that you think was going on inside the young man.

9. How did the father in the story respond to the son's return? What is Jesus telling us in this story about how God feels about us when we stray, and about how we reconnect with Him?

EMBRACING THE TRUTH - 25 MINUTES

LEADER: *The GROUP EXPERIENCE leads into this "Embracing the Truth" time to help group members move from head knowledge to heart knowledge in regard to (a) connection with the Father, (b) wholehearted focus, and (c) the power of truth and right choices. This should be a good discussion, but be sure to save time for important decision points in the "Connecting" segment.*

LEADER INSTRUCTIONS FOR GROUP EXPERIENCE: *Show the video clip from the movie* Indiana Jones and the Last Crusade, *in which Indiana and those working against him must go through a deadly passage to enter the cave where the Holy Grail is hidden. This scene ends after the two men make their choices. This clip begins at the end of scene 33 and runs into scene 34; from 1:42:27 to 1:49:08 minutes on the DVD. (Queue up this scene before your session.)*

1. Were the path and struggles in the passageway any different for Indiana than for the others? What things did you see that made the difference in his getting through to the other side?

2. What did you see as the driving desires for Indy? What were the distorted desires that were driving the general and his accomplice?

3. What role did connection with his father play in how Indy's story turned out? How did Jones view and use truth in his journey?

4. What impact did the characters' choices have in the outcome of their stories? In what ways does your own story mimic this one, and how could this be different for you as you go on from here?

As we started this session, we talked about "unsolved mysteries." In each of your lives, you have unsolved mysteries and unwritten endings. The question is whether you'll just give up and let somebody else or the enemy control you, desperately struggle on your own, or choose to turn over the control of your story—your life—to God.

13 As a father has compassion on his children, so the LORD has compassion on those who fear Him. 14 For He knows what we are made of, remembering that we are dust.

PSALM 103:13-14 HCSB

8 By grace you have been saved through faith; and that not of yourselves, it is the gift of God; 9 not as a result of works, so that no one may boast.

EPHESIANS 2:8-9 NASB

12 Work out your salvation with fear and trembling; 13 for it is God who is at work in you to will and to work for His good pleasure.

PHILIPPIANS 2:12B-13 NASB

5. As you read Psalm 103:13-14, do you think God is surprised by our failures? How does He respond to them?

6. Does Philippians 2:12 say, "Work for your salvation"? What might "WORK OUT your salvation" mean when Ephesians 2:8-9 clearly explains that salvation is God's free gift that we receive through faith in Jesus?

7. Does turning our lives and wills over to God mean we just kick our life's engine into neutral and sit back? Does it mean we're immune from believing lies, making poor choices, and being trapped in addictions? Please explain.

CONNECTING - 15 MINUTES

Each of us comes to a moment of decision. Our options are to get real, or sink back into a shell of denial. In a truly Redemptive Community people find a safe place to be authentic and honest. We accept each other for where we are in our journeys, and lend strength.

WHO WILL WRITE THE REST OF YOUR STORY?

Always remember the three forces that want to drag us down—the world, our distorted passions, and our enemy. These three work together to make you believe you've lost the right to choose, forfeited your right as a child of God, and become hopelessly trapped.

For those of us who have never really put their faith in Jesus and trusted Him for our salvation, Jesus offers this promise and this warning:

To all who did receive Him [Jesus], He gave them the right to be children of God, to those who believe in His name.

JOHN 1:12 HCSB

The god of this age has blinded the minds of unbelievers, so that they cannot see the light of the gospel [good news] of the glory of Christ, who is the image of God.

2 CORINTHIANS 4:4 NIV

1. According to John 1:12, what are the two things we have to do for Jesus to give us all the rights as children of God (including salvation and His divinely powerful weapons)?

2. Who is the "god of this age" 2 Corinthians 4:4 warns about, and what's his strategy?

Here is Jesus' truth for those of us who have already put our faith in Him, receiving Him as our Rescuer and Savior, but are fighting to get life on track:

¹² Brothers, we are not obligated to the flesh to live according to the flesh, ¹³ for if you live according to the flesh, you are going to die. But if by the Spirit you put to death the deeds of the body, you will live. ¹⁴ All those lead by God's Spirit are God's sons. ¹⁵ For you did not receive a spirit of slavery to fall back into fear, but you received the Spirit of adoption, by whom we cry out, "Abba, Father!"

ROMANS 8:12-15 HCSB

If anyone is in Christ, he is a new creation; the old has gone, the new has come.

2 CORINTHIANS 5:17 NIV

3. The "flesh" is distorted passions and habits we still haul around. Can and do Christ-followers "live according to the flesh"? What choices do we have according to Romans 8:12-15?

4. If we who are "in Christ" are a "new creation" (2 Corinthians 5:17), why do we fall back into slavery to the "flesh"? How can we live out of our new heart as a new creation? (See Romans 8:14-15.)

Knocking at the Door

Close your eyes and envision your heart as a house in the country. It has a large door, and Jesus is standing outside. He won't barge in and push Himself on you because He loves you and respects your free will. He's patient in waiting for you and says:

²⁰ Here I am! I stand at the door and knock. If anyone hears my voice and opens the door, I will come in and eat with him, and he with me. ²¹ To him who overcomes, I will give the right to sit with me on my throne, just as I overcame and sat down with my Father on his throne.

REVELATION 3:20-21 NIV

He speaks these words specifically to His followers, but He also calls in the same way to unbelieving people He's trying so hard to connect with.

5. Identify where you are in this third step of the journey: Making a decision to turn my life and will over to the care of God. Be honest with yourself.

1	2	3	4	5	6	7	8	9	10
I'm not sure I really trust God/Jesus, yet		I'm ready to receive Jesus & be adopted by my Father			I've received Jesus, but the spirit of slavery is overpowering me			I'm ready to learn to live as a New Creation	

Is there any way that this group can support you practically in specific ways this week as you face the addictions in your life? How can we pray for you today?

My Prayer Requests & Needs:

My Group's Prayer Requests & Needs:

Closing Recovery Prayer:

Jesus — it's amazing to think that You, the King of all creation, care about each one of us individually, and patiently knock at the door of our hearts. Help each of us to invite You into our stories and to offer our lives and wills to Your care and power. Give each of us a personal encounter with You this week. Help us look ahead to life on the other side and ... choose wisely.

LEADER: *Let group members know that you'll make yourself available to discuss any personal questions about knowing Jesus personally. Continue to encourage group members to find an accountability partner within the group (same-sex partners unless they struggle with homosexuality). Accountability partners should contact each other during the week to support each other, especially when temptations are strong.*

Taking it Home

LEADER: *Strongly encourage everyone to continue their decision process at home throughout the week, using the "My Story" questions and daily journaling. This is a pivotal step and it's important the people don't gloss over it. People of faith are likely to assume they have this step covered, but that is often not the case because many Christ-followers are not living in freedom. Ask group members to review Steps 1 and 2 as they wrestle with Step 3.*

It's up to you to make what we're discussing your own. Nobody will tell you this process is easy, but it's got to be better than living with addictions and the mess it makes of life.

MY STORY: Trust in the Holy Spirit to open your eyes & heart as you write.

1. What major distorted desires seem to be driving my insane behaviors and destructive habit patterns?

As we walk through this process with God, we'll want to turn over every hurt and every thing that has control of our hearts. To find freedom, we'll also need to give Him every expectation and every disappointment.

2. What specific areas of my life and my will am I really ready to turn over to God?

3. What specific areas of my life do I fear or worry about turning over to God? What am I really concerned about? What am I afraid to lose?

NOTE: It's important to find someone in the group or outside of it that you're beginning to feel comfortable opening up to. Please consider asking this person to become an accountability partner that you could open with and also encourage.

QUESTIONS TO TAKE TO GOD:

When you ask God a question, expect His Spirit to respond to your heart and spirit. Be careful not to rush it or manufacture an answer. Don't write down what you think the "right answer" is. Don't turn the Bible into a reference book or spiritual encyclopedia. Just pose your question to God and wait on Him to answer. Focus on listening to God, and be sure to record what you hear and sense He is saying to you.

   ✳ God, how do You see me and feel about me personally? How would You react, and how might my life change if I came home like the prodigal son?

＊ God, You know me better than I know myself. Would You reveal the deep, good desires in my heart that have been distorted in my addiction? Help me to see the real, good unfulfilled desires and how You satisfy these.

IDEAS FOR YOUR DAILY JOURNAL: (as simple as a spiral notebook)
- Distorted desires that I see popping up through the week
- Times when I sensed God's presence and His personal touches in my life
- Thoughts and feelings about God, other people, my life situation, and myself
- Lies I've been believing, struggles, and temporary setbacks
- Times I'm living as a New Creation, embracing the God-given desires of my new heart (even small steps in this direction are huge!)

I know I have a long way to go, but I'm ready to take Step 3: I make a decision to turn my life and will over to the care of God more and more as I know Him deeper.

I have received Jesus as the true Savior of my life and have joined God's family.

Signed _____ Date: _____

I have opened the door for Jesus to take control of my life and teach me to live according to the Spirit, as a New Creation, living out the desires of my new heart and not from the distorted, deceitful desires of the flesh.

Signed _____ Date: _____

The DNA of Our Addictions (Step 4)

Group Progress Check

Step 3 in our recovery is key. Each person will progress through the 12 Steps at his or her OWN PACE, and that's okay! It's time to take a poll of your group. If the majority of your group is not yet ready to complete Steps 1-3, it's wise to delay Step 4. Instead, spend this session reviewing Steps 1-3 and discussing how people are feeling, and in what ways they might be wrestling with the first three steps.

Breaking the Ice - 15 minutes

LEADER: *Because this step is very difficult for some people, start out very light-hearted and fun. Encourage each person to respond to the "Breaking the Ice" questions. Help him or her to open up with their perspectives and questions. It helps to ask people by name how they would respond to a particular question. You may skip one of these icebreakers, if needed, to manage your time.*

1. **Hard to Swallow:** What is the weirdest food you can recall eating? Out of all the stuff you've tried to eat, describe the most difficult.

2. Has there ever been an incredibly tough challenge you took on and succeeded in? Describe it briefly for the group.

3. DNA evidence has become a huge tool in crime solving. Why has it become such a focus? What's it's value?

OPENING PRAYER:

God, help us begin to see our life's story from Your perspective throughout this week. As we begin to examine ourselves, make us aware of life-shaping events, well-worn patterns of behavior, and lies we've accepted as truth. These things and more will help us understand the DNA of our addictions.

IN STEP 3: We recognized the tension and distinction between our old habit patterns and the New Creation God makes us when we trust in Jesus. In understanding the heart and power of God, we discussed the vital step of deciding to turn our hearts fully to God so He can write our story to healing, freedom, and wholeness.

IN STEP 4: Now that we've set our course with God in the center of our story, the Holy Spirit can lead us to truth. Our next step is to begin to uncover the DNA of our addictions—the driving forces we identify as we look backward, outward, and inward.

OBJECTIVES FOR THIS STEP:

- Reflect on the power of honesty and truth in our lives
- Begin to understand the factors that drive our obsessive thinking and addictions
- Learn how to map the DNA of our addictions
- Allow the Holy Spirit to reveal the underlying causes of our bondage
- Begin to release the stranglehold of the past, lies of the enemy, secrets, and denial

DISCOVERING THE TRUTH - 40 MINUTES

LEADER: *This session will include a lot of information and instructions to group members for mapping the DNA of their addictions. Be sure to invite people to read the Bible passages. Be sure to leave time for "Embracing the Truth" and "Connecting" segments that follow.*

Today we approach the first step in "Searching Myself" from our Recovery Map: TAKE INVENTORY: We make a searching and fearless inventory of our lives and our hearts ... to map the DNA of our addictions.

Recovery Map

STARTING WITH	1	1. Admit your need
DECISION	2	2. Find new power
	3	3. Make a decision
SEARCHING	**4**	**4. Take inventory**
MY SELF	5	5. Admit your addiction to others
	6	6. Prepare for change
SEEKING HEALING	7	7. Ask God to restore & redeem life
& CHANGE	8	8. Identify resentments & offenses
	9	9. Make amends
STICKING	10	10. Be preventative
WITH IT	11	11. Stay connected with God
	12	12. Share your story

THE DNA OF ADDICTIONS

DNA in our bodies is essentially the mini-computer programming in the innermost part of each cell, which determines how that cell will behave. If the DNA is hurt as it's being formed, or is traumatized by some outside force, the function of the cell will be damaged. The DNA of our addictions is the programming in our innermost selves that drives how we approach life. Defective DNA can lead to addictions and a host of other problems that can keep us from living in freedom as God intended.

DEFECTIVE DNA

In Step 2, we unveiled the forces at work in our lives: the fallen world we live in, our distorted passions, and our enemy. These forces affect the heart DNA in our innermost being, deep below the surface in the part of ourselves we seldom see. This is where the battle rages for our hearts.

You [God] desire truth in the innermost being, and in the hidden part You will make me know wisdom.
PSALM 51:6 NASB

1. What does Psalm 51:6 point out as the center for our spiritual DNA? What has become defective there, and how can it be corrected?

LEADER: *Share the following the "Captive Heart Model" and "Critical Path to Healing." Read the explanations in this section and don't worry if you don't have all the answers. Each person's journey and part in the larger story is unique. Only God has all the answers. Involve group members by asking for volunteers to read.*

DEFECTIVE DNA IN OUR LIVES

Once we begin to recognize the battle being waged for our hearts and our souls, the pain and struggles in our lives come into focus. The enemy strategically works to distort our identity—our perception of who we are. This distortion keeps us out of the glory we were intended to live in, and the intimacy God wants us to share with Him.

Although God has already sealed Satan's fate through Jesus' death and resurrection, Satan is still "prowling around" (1 Peter 5:8), and using his primary tactic of deception to take us out! He wants to make us believe that God is not good, to put his twisted perspective on every event, to wreak pain and havoc in our lives, and ultimately to destroy us. Let's look at the common threads in our life stories that can distort our heart DNA.

* Strategic ARROWS are launched into our lives create WOUNDS:
  A difficult loss ... Painful circumstances ... Traumatic event ... Neglect ...

* Our WOUNDS become infected with LIES or false beliefs:
  "God has abandoned me" ... "I'm a failure" ... "It's up to me to look out for me" ...

* Satan continues to repeat LIES until we make AGREEMENTS to accept them as truth:
  "I <u>am</u> on my own now" ... "There <u>is</u> no hope" ... I <u>can't</u> live without this" ...

* Once AGREEMENTS are made VOWS are soon to follow:
  "I will never again ..." ... "From now on, I will always ..."

* False agreements and vows feed our FALSE SELF:
  Our distorted belief about who we are ... The person we falsely assume we are (remember the Lion King's revelation – "You're more than you've become.")

CAPTIVE HEART MODEL

ARROWS launched into our lives create WOUNDS

Wounds get infected with FALSE BELIEFS

We make AGREEMENTS with the repeated lies of the enemy

Agreements turn into VOWS – I'll never ... always

Our FALSE SELF is a distortion of who we are

* Captive Heart Model & Critical Path to Healing developed by Ron Keck.

2. In which of these areas do you feel the greatest amount of bondage? Wounds? Lies or false beliefs? Agreements? Vows? Living out of your false self? Please explain.

THE CRITICAL PATH TO HEALING

In essence, this "Captive Heart Model" shows how the innermost DNA in all of our stories develops.

The "Critical Path to Healing" recognizes that every behavior has a corresponding belief, and that our behavior is a better indicator of what we really believe than our intellectual agreements. We start with the outward behavior and follow it inward to our hearts.

It's important to understand that this model is not necessarily linear. Our stories and our identities can be distorted through any of the five ports in different situations. The "Critical Path to Healing" recognizes that we will likely have to battle in one or more of the following areas to experience God's healing and restoration:

- Identify and renounce the lies that we've embraced
- Break the agreements we've made with the lies and replace them with truth
- Denounce the vows we've made and replace old vows with new ones
- Refuse to live out of our false self and embrace who we really are in Christ

3. Does this "Captive Heart Model" and "Critical Path to Healing" shed any light on your situation? Can you see ways the enemy has exploited your story? Discuss this with the group.

SEPARATING THE REAL ME FROM MY "BLOB"

One of the lies of the enemy is to make us believe we *are* what we *do*, that we are defined by our addictions.

¹⁵ For I do not understand what I am doing, because I do not practice what I want to do, but I do what I hate. ¹⁶ And if I do what I do not want to do, I agree with the law that it is good. ¹⁷ So now I am no longer the one doing it, but it is sin living in me.

ROMANS 7:15-17 HCSB

4. What is the inner struggle Paul is describing in Romans 7:15-16? What does Paul imply about his identity, the truest thing about himself? Whom or what does he conclude is doing these destructive things?

5. Why is it important to distinguish between our who we are and the things we do? What's the danger in connecting our identity with our addictions and failures?

Let's speak the truth together in unison:

"I am image-bearer of God, and loved passionately by Him. When I trusted Jesus, I was adopted as a child of God, with all it's rights and privileges. I am not my addiction. I am a true child of the one true King who struggles with _____."

DIVINELY POWERFUL WEAPON: TRUTH

It's time to begin using those divinely powerful weapons we've talked about! Step 4: Taking Inventory—mapping our addiction and searching our heart—is not easy, but it's powerful. As we make a searching and fearless inventory, we'll begin to bring addictive behaviors, feelings, and beliefs out from the darkness and into the light. We've been bound too long in the shadow world of denial, deception, and half-truths. Looking hard at ourselves would be frightening without the knowledge that God is on our side. God loves us and wants us to be free of denial and deception.

⁶ You [God] desire truth in the innermost being, and in the hidden part You will make me know wisdom ... ⁸ Make me to hear joy and gladness, let the bones which you have broken rejoice. ⁹ Hide Your face from my sins and blot out all my iniquities. ¹⁰ Create in me a clean heart and renew a steadfast spirit within me ... ¹² Restore me to the joy of Your salvation and sustain me with a willing spirit.

PSALM 51:6,8-10,12 NASB

King David wrote Psalm 51 after having an illicit affair with Bathsheba, getting her husband killed to cover it up, and then taking her as his wife.

6. As you read his discussion with God, what turning points do you see in David's attitude about his failures that will allow God to forgive, heal, and restore him? What role do brutal honesty and brokenness play in his restoration?

23 Search me, O God, and know my heart; test me and know my anxious thoughts. 24 See if there is any offensive way in me, and lead me in the way everlasting.

PSALM 139:23-24 NIV

Let us examine and probe our ways, and let us return to the Lord.

LAMENTATIONS 3:40 NASB

12 The word of God is living and active. Sharper than any two-edged sword, it penetrates even to dividing soul and spirit, joints and marrow; it judges the thoughts and attitudes of the heart. 13 Nothing in all creation is hidden from God's sight. Everything is uncovered and laid bare before the eyes of him to whom we must give account.

HEBREWS 4:12-13 NIV

7. What two critical steps did King David take in Psalm 139:23-24 that set the stage for restoration to take place?

8. According to Lamentations 3 and Psalm 139, who does the searching of our life and heart? What is the goal of each search?

9. In what ways can the Holy Spirit make your personal inventory more powerful and insightful than we could ever accomplish on our own? How does that make you feel?

King David took the initiative in his healing and redemption. He chose self-scrutiny. He also set aside denial, and asked for God's divine help and revelation.

EMBRACING THE TRUTH - 20 MINUTES

MAPPING THE DNA OF ADDICTION

As we write out our personal inventory and the story of our addiction, and as we hear the stories of others on this journey with us, we begin to see vital truths emerge:

- Key events that have shaped our lives and addictions
- Deep-rooted pain
- The well-worn paths and ruts we develop to cope
- Destructive and self-defeating behaviors
- False beliefs and powerful vows taken
- Exposure of our false self compared to our true identity in Christ

Many people approach the Step 4 personal inventory as if it was a time to beat themselves up, and be punished by God for all their sins and failures. But while this is not an easy time, the goal is seeking truth and being restored. (Remember the prodigal son.)

3 When I kept silent about my sin, my body wasted away through my groaning all day long. 4 For day and night Your hand was heavy upon me; my vitality was drained away as with the fever heat of summer. 5 I acknowledged my sin to You, and my iniquity I did not hide; I said, "I will confess my transgressions to the LORD"; and You forgave the guilt of my sin.

PSALM 32:1-5 NASB

Psalm 32 is probably the sequel to Psalm 51. King David is reflecting back on his struggles after his adultery, lying, and murder. He shares the outcome of taking inventory of his life, and then laying it all out before God for His scrutiny and forgiveness.

1. What happened when David "kept silent"? Describe the dynamic playing out in you during a time when you've felt like David when he lived in denial, secrecy, and shame?

2. What happened when David brought the truth to light with God? What do you think this journey was like for him?

One goal of mapping the DNA of our addiction is confessing failures and receiving forgiveness and new life from God. But, there's an even more vital goal for our recovery: Transformations!.

Do not conform any longer to the pattern of this world, but be transformed by the renewing of your mind. Then you will be to test and approve what God's will is—his good, pleasing and perfect will.

ROMANS 12:2 NIV

⁴ The weapons we fight with are not the weapons of the world. On the contrary , they have divine power to demolish strongholds. ⁵ We demolish arguments and every pretension that sets itself up against the knowledge of God and we take every thought captive.

2 CORINTHIANS 10:4-5 NIV

¹ Therefore, since we have this ministry [reflecting the glory of God], as we have received mercy, we do not give up. ² Instead, we have renounced shameful secret things, not walking in deceit or distorting God's message, but in God's sight we commend ourselves to every person's conscience by the open display of the truth.

2 CORINTHIANS 4:1-2 HCSB

3. Each of these three passages has the goal of exposing lies we've believed and desires and passions that have been distorted. In each passage, what divinely powerful weapon are we to use and what is it's purpose?

Romans 12:2 –

2 Corinthians 10:4-5 –

2 Corinthians 4:1-2 –

4. We are to reject the "pattern of this world" (Romans 12:2) and demolish "strongholds" (2 Corinthians 10:4). What do these words signify? Give examples.

The battle before us is not quick or easy: Renewing our minds, demolishing strongholds, taking thoughts captive, renouncing secret things, and living out of the desires of our new hearts instead of distorted passions and habits.

How to Map the DNA of Addiction

- **WRITE IT OUT:** Putting the story of your addiction on paper makes it real and allows you to look back for patterns and commons issues. Just write!!

- **BE SPECIFIC:** Be specific in describing your feelings, destructive behaviors, desires, triggers, choices, and the like.

- **FOCUS TO YOUR ADDICTION:** Stay focused on the addiction that binds you so this process is effective and manageable.

- **KEEP IT BALANCED:** At the same time you're capturing character defects, faulty perceptions, and self-destructive behaviors, don't overlook your strengths.

- **TAKE ONE BITE AT A TIME:** How do you eat an elephant? One bite at a time You have a lifetime of hurts, failures, and regrets in your secret basement. You must bring them to the light so they stop decaying in the dark, BUT nobody can haul all that junk up at once. Work with God as He reveals which junk to pull out first.

- **MAKE IT PERSONAL:** While there are things to consider and steps you can take, each person's process will and should be different. Let the Holy Spirit direct you.

ASK GOD TO BRING CLARITY AS YOU REMEMBER

STEP 1: Create some pages in a notebook for the key stages of your life: Early Childhood, Childhood, Teens, Young Adulthood, Single Years, Married Years, etc.

STEP 2: Start with the earliest life stage and write down everything you can remember that might be relevant to your addiction. Let one memory lead to another.

STEP 3: At each stage, be sure to consider the following areas:
- wounds: hurtful events & painful memories
- major transitions & life-changing events
- regular patterns of behavior (well-worn paths & ruts)
- character defects & destructive or self-defeating behaviors
- beliefs about God, life, yourself, and the world around you that are behind your destructive behaviors
- identify any vows you took (I'll always ... I'll never ...)
- personal failures & people we've hurt
- secrets & sources of shame you've kept hidden

STEP 4: Spend time with God as you're writing, asking Him to reveal the true story of your addiction. Let your story evolve.

STEP 5: Ask God to help you compare the various stages of your life to identify common patterns, false beliefs, root causes of your addiction, effects and losses from your addiction, and your deepest longings and questions.

CONNECTING - 20 MINUTES

LEADER INSTRUCTIONS FOR GROUP EXPERIENCE: *Give each group member a spiral bound notebook and 10 minutes to find a quiet spot nearby to write about the DNA of his or her addiction. It will help to have some nice music playing quietly in the background for this time. Offer comfort & encouragement to those who are struggling with the exercise. The goal is to get people comfortable with writing. Call the group back together for your closing.*

[Jesus promises:] [31] *If you continue in My word, you really are My disciples.* [32] *You will know the truth, and the truth will set you free.*

2 JOHN 8:31-32 HCSB

With this encouragement, find a quiet, nearby spot to be alone. Invite God to join you for 10 minutes as you write whatever is at the front of your mind regarding the DNA of your addiction. Don't worry about structure or analysis right now. Just begin to dump from your brain and your heart onto the paper.

Your group leader will call you back together for your closing.

1. How did it go? How did it feel to begin writing some of your story down?

2. How can this group help you and pray for you as you dive into Step 4?

My Prayer Requests & Needs:

My Group's Prayer Requests & Needs:

Closing Recovery Prayer:

God, if You don't go with us, we don't want to go. Bind the enemy in our lives this week so we can clearly see the truth in our stories. Give us the commitment to scrutinize ourselves, and open ourselves to Your scrutiny.

Taking it Home

LEADER: *This week's "Taking it Home" activity is to grab a notebook, invite the Father, Jesus, and the Holy Spirit to join you, and WRITE!*

Look back at page 64 for key points & steps as you begin to map the DNA of your addiction this week. Probe ... Evolve ... Let your story emerge!

I have begun to map the DNA of my addiction.

Signed _____ Date: _____

It has been a journey, but I have now completed my map.

Signed _____ Date: _____

Break the Power of Secrecy (Step 5)

Breaking the Ice - 20 minutes

LEADER INSTRUCTIONS FOR GROUP EXPERIENCE: *Following initial greetings and welcome, show a clip from the movie* Goonies. *There's a scene in which the bad guys catch the little chubby kid, Chunk. They interrogate him trying to find out what happened to the treasure map. When they tell him to "spill your guts, kid," he starts into a true confessions time about all the bad things he did in grade school. The first clip is near the middle of Scene 17 (runs from 51:54 to 52:49 minutes on the DVD. (Queue up this scene before your session.) We recommend also showing the continuation at the beginning of Scene 20 (runs from 58:09 to 59:20 minutes) on the DVD.*

In the movie *Goonies*, a group of kids is trying to find a pirate treasure, but a nasty woman and her two grown sons will do almost anything to get it. They catch the little guy named Chuck, and it's true confessions time. Following the movie clip, discuss these questions:

1. As a group, make a list of the "top ten most difficult things about surviving grade school" (David Letterman style). These should be pretty funny. Some things that may make the list are warm curdled milk at lunch and not getting cooties from girls.

2. If you had to confess a childhood "sin"—something you never told your parents you did—what would you confess?

3. If you could call "do-over" and get a fresh start to your life that would erase all the mistakes you've made, and wipe out all the times you've hurt others, would you do it? Discuss your answer.

4. What approach are you taking in Step 4 to map the DNA of your addiction? What are you finding difficult? What can you do to push through it in the next week or two?

Opening Prayer:

Jesus, Hebrews 4:15 says You've been tempted in every way that each of us has, but You are God and have the power to beat it all. Unleash that power in our lives as we admit our addictions to You and ourselves. Give us courage as, together, we break the power of secrecy.

In Step 4:

We began to uncover the DNA of our addictions, as we revealed the Critical Path to Healing, and the divinely powerful weapon of truth. We discussed the battle for our minds and hearts, and learned the goals and process for mapping our own addictions.

In Step 5:

We all have hidden things and secrets. The enemy knows if he can keep us in hiding and isolated, then we'll remain captive to the "darkness." He hates truth; he hates light; he hates God; he hates community; and he hates you. We're not going to "spill our guts" like Chunk in the *Goonies*, but we must break the power of secrecy to find freedom.

Objectives for this Step:

- Understand the power of openness in our lives
- Embrace the need bring the shadows of secrecy into the "light"
- Learn to break the power of secrecy
- Begin to move from isolation into the healing environment of redemptive community
- Begin to live beyond ourselves to accept and build one another up

Discovering the Truth - 35 minutes

LEADER: *In the initial part of "Discovering the Truth," you'll discuss the power of openness. You may ask various group members to read explanations and Bible passages. This discussion on openness continues into discovery about "light" and "darkness." Then, you'll then transition to breaking the power of secrecy. Keep things moving through this section and also "Embracing the Truth." You'll want to leave plenty of time for sharing stories in the "Connecting" segment today .*

We're making great progress! Today we approach the fifth step in our Recovery Map: ADMIT YOUR ADDICTION TO OTHERS: We admit to God, ourselves, and another human being the exact nature of our failures, and the burdens we've been carrying alone.

RECOVERY MAP

STARTING WITH	1	1. Admit your need
DECISION	2	2. Find new power
	3	3. Make a decision
SEARCHING	4	4. Take inventory
MY SELF	**5**	**5. Admit your addiction to others**
	6	6. Prepare for change
SEEKING HEALING	7	7. Ask God to restore & redeem life
& CHANGE	8	8. Identify resentments & offenses
	9	9. Make amends
STICKING	10	10. Be preventative
WITH IT	11	11. Stay connected with God
	12	12. Share your story

We've discussed that an addiction is any self-defeating behavior that we can't stop despite its adverse consequences. Our false beliefs, distorted desires, and well-worn paths of behavior create ruts that make life unmanageable. Even after we've surrendered our lives to Jesus, we still carry baggage from our past. We can continue to bury our story deep inside, denying its importance and the emotions it contains, or we can unpack our baggage. That's what we're doing in Steps 4, 5, and 6.

DIVINELY POWERFUL WEAPON: BRUTAL HONESTY

It's very important to name our "drug of choice." If you can't name your addiction and call it what it is, then you're not going to get well. But naming our addictions only takes us so far. It's one thing to admit our addictions, it's another to reveal our stories to someone else.

Laying aside every falsehood, speak the truth each of you with his neighbor, for we are all members of one another.

EPHESIANS 4:25 NASB

Confess your sins to one another and pray for one another, so that you may be healed. The intense prayer of the righteous is very powerful.

JAMES 5:16 HCSB

1. The Greek word for "falsehood" (Ephesians 4:25) used in the original language of the New Testament literally refers to the masks that were worn in Greek theatre. What does this verse say about our need to be real with each other?

2. Why do you think we try to hide our hurt and pain.? Why is it so difficult to remove our masks and be real with each other?

3. What motivation is given in Ephesians 4:25 and James 5:16 for taking the risk and being real? What do you think would happen if we'd risk being real with God, ourselves, and others in the journey of recovery with us?

There's great power in brutal honesty about our addictions. It's another one of those divinely powerful weapons. Once we've said it, others now know and there's no going back. We've come out of the shadows and into the light. It's the difference between living a lie and living the truth. Once our masks are down, and we're being real with each other, we can move into the task of helping each other find healing and freedom.

LIGHT AND DARKNESS

[8] *For you were once darkness [before faith in Jesus], but now you are light in the Lord. Walk as children of light—* [9] *for the fruit of the light results in all goodness, righteousness, and truth—* [10] *discerning what is pleasing to the Lord.* [11] *Don't participate in the fruitless works of darkness, but instead, expose them.* [13] *Everything exposed by the light is made clear.* [14] *For what makes everything clear is light.*

EPHESIANS 5:8-11,13-14A HCSB

Do not go on passing judgment before the time, but wait until the Lord comes who will both bring to light the things hidden in the darkness and disclose the motives of men's hearts; and then each man's praise will come to him from the Lord.

1 CORINTHIANS 4:5 NASB

4. The Bible says God is "light" and Jesus is the "Light of the World." According to Ephesians 5:8-11, how do children of light walk?

5. What reasons does God give for us to avoid the darkness, and expose the dark and secret things in our lives (and hearts) to light and truth? (See Ephesians 5:13-14; 1 Corinthians 4:5.)

BREAKING THE POWER OF SECRECY

² You are the God of my refuge ... Why must I go about in sorrow because of the enemy's oppression? ³ Send Your light and Your truth; let them lead me. Let them bring me to Your holy mountain, to Your dwelling place.

PSALM 43:2-3 HCSB

6. Too often we hide from God because we believe lies about His goodness and care for us. What picture does the psalmist paint of God in Psalm 43:2-3? What two things can lead us out of the enemy's oppression into God's presence for relationship and safety?

⁵ God is light, and there is absolutely no darkness in Him. ⁶ If we say, "We have fellowship with Him," and walk in darkness, we are lying and are not practicing the truth. ⁷ But if we walk in the light as He is in the light, we have fellowship with one another, and the blood of Jesus his Son cleanses us from all sin. ⁸ If we say, "We have no sin," we are deceiving ourselves, and the truth is not is us. ⁹ If we confess our sins, He is faithful and righteous to forgive us of our sins and to cleanse us from all unrighteousness.

1 JOHN 1:5B-9 HCSB

7. According to 1 John 1:5-9, what relationships are broken when we are walking in darkness and false beliefs rather than following God? Conversely, if we admit or confess our sins to God, what does He promise (verses 7 and 9)?

We've been learning that the villain in our story wants to use hurts (arrows) and lies to keep us separated from God and oppressed by our addictions. We've also grasped the truth that God knows all about our struggles and "secrets," and He's longing to help us find freedom and redeem our lives. God only needs us to confess our addictions and invite His Spirit to take the lead in our stories. Now, let's consider confession to people.

16 Make this your common practice: Confess your sins to each other and pray for each other so that you can live together whole and healed. The prayer of a person living right with God is something powerful to be reckoned with. ... 19 My dear friends, if you know people who have wandered off from God's truth, don't write them off. Go after them. 20 Get them back and you will have rescued precious lives from destruction and prevented an epidemic of wandering away from God.

JAMES 5:16,9-20 MESSAGE

8. What good could come of telling our life's stories to another person we can trust? How necessary is that, really? Reread James 5:16,19-20, and then as a group list the advantages of admitting our addictions and sharing our stories.

9. If I open up and share the story of my life and addiction with people in the group, what's the worst that could really happen?
   - ☐ Someone may condemn or criticize me.
   - ☐ I may be terribly embarrassed.
   - ☐ It's so bad, they may turn away from me in rejection.
   - ☐ Someone might use the information against me.
   - ☐ One word: Gossip
   - ☐ I may dehydrate from the sweat and my heart may explode!
   - ☐ Other: _____.

CAUTION: Brutal honesty about ourselves is a powerful weapon, but we must be careful to be selective about what we share with whom. There's great release and freedom in being able open up and not hold back with people that understand our situation and are able to keep a confidence. Brutal honesty about our addictions outside of that close circle could create large misunderstandings and even anxiety or withdrawal.

Embracing the Truth - 15 minutes

Hertz Doughnut?

When you were kid did you ever have some joker come up to you and ask, Do you want a hertz doughnut"? After you said, "Sure," he slugged you in the arm and hollered, "It hertz doughnut?" Some people look at sharing their stories like getting a hertz doughnut, but it's more like a life preserver than a doughnut.

Nobody denies it ... admitting to being controlled by food, sex, cocaine, alcohol, even jogging is not easy. We fear losing face, giving up our illusions of control, and opening the flood gates of bad feelings such as shame, humiliation, guilt, anger, and worthlessness. Most of us have lived in denial so long that it's hard to face up to specific, negative traits in ourselves, and to the wrongs we've done to ourselves and others.

Step 5 of admitting our addictions is a huge step toward healing. Everybody's here with some kind of addiction, so let's encourage and support each other in the process.

Divinely Powerful Weapon: Community

We can and need to tell our story to people we trust. This step has a purpose way beyond reopening old wounds – we're here for recovery, freedom, and healing. Healing occurs best within the context of community and relationships.

9 Two are better than one because they have a good reward for their efforts. 10 For if either falls, his companion can lift him up; but pity the one who falls without another to life him up. 11 Also, if two lie down together, they can keep warm; but how can one person alone keep warm? 12 And if somebody overpowers one person, two can resist him. A cord of three strands is not easily broken.

ECCLESIASTES 4:9-12 HCSB

1. According to Ecclesiastes 4:10-12, what three situations can we find ourselves in when we try to go it alone? In each case, how would it help to have a friend or two with you?

2. Looking at the end of Ecclesiastes 4:12, we see that three people are even better than two to help us up when we've fallen ethically, spiritually, or physically. In your experience, why is this true? How can you create a life with a "cord of three strands"?

24 *Let us be concerned about one another in order to promote love and good works,* 25 *not staying away from our meetings, as some habitually do, but encouraging each other, and all the more as you see the day drawing near.*

HEBREWS 10:24-25 HCSB

25 *The way God designed our bodies is a model for understanding our lives together as a church [or other redemptive community]: every part dependent on every other part, the parts we mention and the parts we don't, the parts we see and the parts we don't.* 26 *If one part hurts, every other part is involved in the hurt, and in the healing. If on part flourishes, ever other part enters into the exuberance.*

1 CORINTHIANS 12:25-26 MESSAGE

3. What benefits come out of belonging to a community according to Hebrews 10:24-25 and 1 Corinthians 12:25-26? Which of these is most appealing to you?

4. Do you have or have you had a real, deep friendship based on openness and trust? How does it make you feel when somebody knows who you really are and still wants to be your friend?

The people in our group have come together at this time to deal with issues that are essentially the same. We've all become slaves to some kind of addiction, and so we are uniquely equipped to help one another. We can be a healing force in other's lives if we:

• Provide a safe environment where confidences are kept

• Give each other opportunities to share our stories and have others really care and listen

• Act as "truth mirrors" to help each other see our true selves, not the masks we wear, nor our insecure, distorted beliefs about other people, God, and ourselves

• Offer acceptance without condemnation (Jesus said to a mob after a woman caught in prostitution, "Let him who is without sin cast the first stone.")

• Lend each other support and encouragement, but also loving accountability

5. What are some ways that we can "spur" each other on to "love and good deeds" (Hebrews 10:24)? What are some things we can do to be good listeners, and yet give the "right word at the right time" (Proverbs 25:11-12)?

CONNECTING - 20 MINUTES

IMPORTANT NOTE FOR THIS SESSION AND THE NEXT:

Please realize that this "Connecting" time will NOT be fully completed today. Plan to use your next meeting or two as a continuation of this step of sharing your stories within the group. Allow people time to share and use the group as a "truth mirror," but set a pace so everyone gets a turn.

STORY-TELLING: WATCH THE CRITICAL PATH TO HEALING

In Session 4, we looked at the "Captive Heart Model" as a way address our addictions:

* Captive Heart Model & Critical Path to Healing developed by Ron Keck.

The path to healing may not be a simple linear path. As you share your stories, help each other to recognize the wounds ... false beliefs ... agreements ... vows ... and emergence of the false self.

STORY-TELLING: CONNECTING THE DOTS

Connecting the dots in your story from present behavior back to your wounds, beliefs, and agreements, and vows can reveal underlying issues and help you understand some of what drives your addictions. When this happens you are most apt to stop casting blame and making excuses. Arrows in your lives can come from hurtful treatment by others, neglect that can be very damaging, awful situations, and even self-inflicted sabotage.

Watch for those distorted desires and well-worn patterns of behavior you keep repeating. Dig for what keep turning you away from God, who alone can fill the desires of your heart.

STORY-TELLING: KEY COMPONENTS

When you share your story, be sure to include these key elements:

- CHARACTERS: heroes, villains, and key people who had good or bad impacts

- MAJOR TRANSITIONS and life-changing events

- RECURRING THEMES: well-worn paths and ruts you keep dropping into, distorted desires, self-perceptions, "drug of choice," people, and places

- CHARACTER DEFECTS and destructive or self-defeating behaviors

- HEALING PATH elements: wounds ... false beliefs ... agreements ... vows ... and emergence of the false self

- PERSONAL FAILURES and people whom I have hurt

- ADMISSION PROGRESS: How are you doing in getting your full story on paper? How are you doing at admitting things to God and yourself?

- INVITATION: Have you invited Jesus into your story? How engaged is He?

You must realize the purpose of Steps 4 and 5 are not to further victimize us. The goal is not to drive nails deeper into your pain. You're searching for the toxic behaviors that were born out of your personal wound.

GROUP EXPERIENCE: STORY-TELLING MAP

Today we're going to begin something really exciting. We get to move beyond a "hertz doughnut" into the beginning of healing! Your group leader will pass out POSTER BOARDS and COLORED MARKERS for your maps. Here's how this works. Each of you will use your poster boards and markers to create a picture that maps out the key points of your addiction story.

Give it you own personal flare and be creative. You may draw a roadmap with destinations or speed traps identified along the way. You might depict a mountain you've climbed, indicating where the barriers have been. Maybe it's a wheel with spokes. Don't sweat your inability to create a masterpiece. Anything you create will be perfect for what we're doing. Just open you heart and mind, and let it flow onto your poster!

LEADER: *Model the assignment by showing your drawing and sharing your story before this exercise. NOTE: Make sure you've brought enough markers and large sheets of paper or posters with you for the whole group. The next page provides space to take notes that might help the story-teller. Allow only 10 minutes for drawing the maps.* **Ask as many to share stories as you have time for today.**

Notes from Our Story-Telling

LEADER: *Stop individual story-telling leaving a few minutes to close your session. Be very affirming of those who shared and congratulate everyone on taking steps forward by creating a map.*

IMPORTANT NOTE: *It may be wise to collect the posters so people don't have to remember to bring them back. Tell group members they are free to create a new poster at home to share during the next meeting or two. Encourage everyone to attend the upcoming meeting(s) that will focus on completing the group story-telling experience. Remind them that we're all in this together.*

GROUP PROGRESS CHECK

Steps 4 & 5 in our recovery are vital and should NOT be rushed. Each person will progress through the 12 steps at his or her OWN PACE - that's okay! BUT, if the majority of your group is not yet ready to complete Steps 4-5, it's wise to delay Step 6, and allow group members to continue mapping the DNA of their addictions and sharing the highlights of their stories with the group. IDEA: You may try setting aside a group meeting to work on the individual maps, as you and other leaders act as coaches.

How can this group hold you up in prayer today and through this week? What practical support, or accountability needs can this group help you with this week?

MY PRAYER REQUESTS & NEEDS:

MY GROUP'S PRAYER REQUESTS & NEEDS:

CLOSING RECOVERY PRAYER:

Dear God, it's so amazing to realize that Your heart aches for the pain that each of us has been through, and that You long to enter our story, bringing Your love, forgiveness, power, and hope. Thanks for bringing each person in this group to play a role in helping others here find healing. Help us persevere in our personal inventory.

Taking it Home

LEADER: *This week's "Taking it Home" activity it to grab your notebook again. Invite the Father, Jesus, and Holy Spirit to join you, and KEEP WRITING!*

STEP 4 CONTINUED:
LOOK BACK AT PAGE 64 FOR KEY POINTS & STEPS AS YOU CONTINUE TO MAP THE DNA OF YOUR ADDICTION THIS WEEK.

I have begun to map the DNA of my addiction.

Signed _____ Date: _____

It has been a journey, but I now have completed my map.

Signed _____ Date: _____

STEP 5:
Once you have pretty much completed mapping the DNA of your addiction, Step 5 requires you to find one of two trusted friends, and then spend several hours sharing your DNA map. The point of this is to admit the exact nature of your addiction(s), as well as all you've learned in completing your map in Step 4. The results will be (1) you will have broken the enslaving power of secrecy; (2) you will have someone to share the hurts, failures, and burdens you've carried lone for so long; and (3) you will gain new insights as you share, and as your listener gives you feedback at points to help you connect the dots.

Who in the group am I beginning to feel most comfortable with and could open up with

one on one or in a small group? _____

I have determined the person(s) with whom I'm going to share my in-depth story.

Signed _____ Date: _____

New Things Have Come! (Step 6)

Breaking the Ice - 10 minutes

> **LEADER:** *We are about half way through the 12 steps in our Recovery Map. By now, your group should be connecting well and supporting each other move toward recovery. The group is now used to deeper discussions, but start out with some lighthearted "Breaking the Ice" questions.*

1. Think about one of the coolest new things you can remember receiving. Describe it to the group.

2. Which of the following Beatle's songs best describes where you presently are in your journey? Tell why.
   - ☐ "The Long and Winding Road" - It seems I'll just never get there
   - ☐ "Here Comes the Sun" - Tomorrow is looking really promising!
   - ☐ "Help! I Need Somebody" - I'm ready to get an accountability partner
   - ☐ "Sgt. Pepper's Lonely Heart Club Band" - I still feel like I'm hanging out
   - ☐ "Come Together Right Now" - I feel this group is going to help pull me through
   - ☐ "Hard Day's Night" - I've been working at this like a dog!
   - ☐ Other: _____

3. Have you completed and signed Step 4 and/or 5? If you did, share with the group how you feel about that? If not, share something you're wrestling with?

4. How hard has it been to find a person you feel comfortable sharing with about your addiction and your in-depth story?

OPENING PRAYER:

Jesus, it has been a "long and winding road" for each of us. But you're no stranger to pain and struggle. You endured shame, beatings, exhaustion, overwhelming stress, isolation from the Father, and death. You've literally been to hell and back on our behalf. Who better to lead us in this process to healing? Please give us fresh sense of Your presence today

IN STEP 5:
We began to break the power of secrecy and embraced the divinely powerful weapons of brutal honesty and community. We shared key parts of our stories with this group, and more importantly, we admitted to at least one other person the exact nature of our addictions and the details of our stories. We have all made significant progress!

IN STEP 6:
We'll prepare our hearts and minds for change. We all need to see change in our lives – that's why we're here. We'll discuss what it means to be a New Creation, how we resist change, and the need to take our deepest thirsts to God. Then, it's time to choose. Are we ready to take unfamiliar, maybe scary paths that lead to healing and life?

OBJECTIVES FOR THIS STEP:

- Accept that we're New Creations in Christ, with new hearts, and hope for a new future
- Recognize and deal with our resistance to change
- Embrace the need to wrestle with God over our questions and struggles
- Realize that Jesus alone can satisfy our deepest desires, heal our hurts, and rescue us from our addictions
- Choose the unfamiliar, sometimes scary paths that lead to healing and life

DISCOVERING THE TRUTH - 40 MINUTES

LEADER: *In the initial part of "Discovering the Truth," you'll discuss what it means to be a New Creation in Christ. You may ask various group members to read explanations and Bible passages. Then you'll discuss resistance to change, and help the group understand how Jesus alone can satisfy our deepest thirst and desires. Leave time for the "Embracing the Truth" and "Connecting" segments.*

Step 6 is often overlooked or passed by quickly, but it's an important part of our Recovery Map: PREPARE FOR CHANGE: We become entirely ready to have God forgive, restore, and redeem our lives, and help us to live out of the new desires of our new heart.

RECOVERY MAP

STARTING WITH	I	1. Admit your need
DECISION	2	2. Find new power
	3	3. Make a decision
SEARCHING	4	4. Take inventory
MY SELF	5	5. Admit your addiction to others
	6	**6. Prepare for change**
SEEKING HEALING	7	7. Ask God to restore & redeem life
& CHANGE	8	8. Identify resentments & offenses
	9	9. Make amends
STICKING	10	10. Be preventative
WITH IT	11	11. Stay connected with God
	12	12. Share your story

There's no doubt that following our Recovery Map has taken many of us places we never dreamed we'd go. We're beginning to get out away from our comfort zones now.
This path we're taking is unfamiliar and even scary. But we've made great progress, and we're still in this together!

NEW EVERYTHING

Too often we define ourselves as the sum of all our failures. We get blinded to who we really are and how God sees us after we've placed our trust in Jesus alone to rescue and redeem us.

[17] Therefore, if anyone is in Christ, he is a new creation; the old has gone, the new has come! [18] All this is from God, who reconciled us to himself through Christ and gave us the ministry of reconciliation.

2 CORINTHIANS 5:17-18 NIV

[God foretelling about the New Covenant:] ²⁵ I will sprinkle clean water on you, and you will be clean; I will cleanse you from all your filthiness and from all your idols. ²⁶ Moreover, I will give you a new heart and put a new spirit within you; and I will remove the heart of stone from your flesh and give you a heart of flesh. ²⁷ I will put my Spirit within you and cause you to walk in My statutes, and you will be careful to follow My ordinances. ... ²⁸ you will be My people , and I will be your God.

EZEKIEL 36:25-28 NASB

1. Who becomes a "New Creation" according to 2 Corinthians 5:17-18? What has happened to the old things (our desires, inclinations, nature)?

2. According to Ezekiel 36:25-28, what key changes does God make in our lives when we become a New Creation in Christ?

3. So, if Christians become new, and have new hearts and spirits, then why are we still such a mess, at the mercy of "idols" (Ezekiel 36:25)—that is our counterfeit lovers or addictions?

Amazingly, God makes us entirely New Creations when we place our faith in Jesus. The only problem is that most of us never experience much of this "new creation." Why?

(1) The enemy has deceived us, telling us God doesn't care and we're nothing.

(2) We continue to live out of the well-worn patterns and ruts in our lives and don't embrace our new hearts and new lives.

(3) We block the work of the Holy Spirit by resisting Him or turning away from God and seeking satisfaction in counterfeit lovers.

(4) All of the above.

RESISTING CHANGE

Living out of our new hearts can be difficult. We're asked to give up beliefs and behaviors that have long dominated our lives. We've admitted how destructive these things are, but when it comes to letting them go, we find out how attached we are to our addictions. They've been our friends and lovers, the place we turn with our pains and desires.

4. As I think about letting go of things I've held onto for so long, which of these are easy for me to release (check the box)? Which are hard to let go (circle these)? Share one or two of these hard ones with the group.

☐ Lies I bought into   ☐ Destructive associations with people/places
☐ Anger about my past   ☐ My addictions (my counterfeit lovers)
☐ Wounds and hurts   ☐ Attitudes about myself and the future
☐ Controlling my goals and plans   ☐ My distorted desires and passions
☐ Bad experiences with people and religion/churches
☐ Other: _____

Resisting change is normal; it's easier to just slide back into our old ruts and continue to live with pain, bondage, and regret. Most of us could never imagine anything good would come from attempting to put God in a headlock and wrestling through our issues with Him. God invites us to wrestle with Him ...

²⁴ Jacob was left alone, and a man [God] wrestled with him until daybreak. ²⁵ When the man saw that He could not defeat him, He struck Jacob's hip as they wrestled and dislocated his hip socket. ²⁶ Then He said to Jacob, "Let Me go, for it is daybreak." But Jacob said, "I will not let You go unless You bless me." ²⁷ "What is your name?" the man asked. "Jacob!" he replied. ²⁸ "Your name will no longer be Jacob," He said. "It will be Israel because you have struggled with God and with men and have prevailed." ²⁹ Then Jacob asked Him, "Please tell me Your name." But He answered, "Why do you ask My name?" And He blessed him there. ³⁰ Jacob then named the place Peniel, "For," [he said,] "I have seen God face to face, and I have been delivered." ³¹ The sun shone on him as he passed by Penuel—limping on his hip.

GENESIS 32:24-31 HCSB

5. According to verse 24, what time of day do you think this bout started?
   On a scale of 1 to 10 how alone do you feel in the late night hours?

1	2	3	4	5	6	7	8	9	10
Completely abandoned									Someone is always available to me

6. How long did Jacob wrestle with God even though he was in severe pain with a dislcated hip? What inner dynamic was needed before this bout would end (verse 26)?

7. Jacob started this fight out of desperation (verse 26). What three blessings did Jacob walk away with after "prevailing" in his struggle (verses 28-29)? What would he have missed if he'd not persisted with God? What would he have taken away if he'd given up?

In the end, God gave Jacob three blessings:
    (1) A new name, signifying a fresh start and identity
    (2) Reconnection and intimacy with God
    (3) "Deliverance" from his pain ... and oh yeah, a limp.

8. How long are you willing to wrestle with God to get what you need? What's it worth to you to get the blessings Jacob received? What might keep you from continuing to fight?

God invites us to wrestle with Him. Psalm 30:5 NASB encourages us saying, "Weeping may last for the night, but a shout of joy comes in the morning."

DIVINELY POWERFUL RESOURCE: LIVING WATER

37 Jesus stood and cried out, saying, "If anyone is thirsty, let him come to Me and drink. 38 "He who believes in Me, as the Scripture said, 'From his innermost being will flow rivers of living water.'"

JOHN 7:37-38 NASB

13 Jesus said, "Everyone who drinks from this water will get thirsty again. 14 But whoever drinks from the water that I will give him will never get thirsty again—ever! In fact, the water I will give him will become a well of water springing up within him for eternal life."

JOHN 4:13-14 HCSB

35 Jesus said, "I am the Bread of Life. The person who aligns with me hungers no more and thirsts no more, ever. 36 I have told you this explicitly because even though you have seen me in action, you really don't believe me. 37 Every person the Father gives me eventually comes running to me. And once that person is with me, I hold on and don't let go.

JOHN 6:35-37 MESSAGE

9. What are the results that Jesus promises in these passages from the Book of John if we take our heart needs and hurts to Him? How does His offer differs from our "pain relievers," "drugs of choice," and counterfeit lovers?

10. Jesus offers each of us a new life, filled with truth, healing, and freedom from our destructive behaviors and addictions ... but we have to fight for it! What does He tell us in these verses that we need to do in order to receive this new life?

Usually we respond according to the distorted desires we have become conditioned to fulfilling. Our "drug of choice" produces a sense of relief, comfort, release, or pleasure. (Examples: take a drink, look at pornography, go shopping, eat chocolate). This pattern is an addiction and it's a trap! To find freedom and life we must turn to Jesus. He alone can heal our pain and fill our hearts with the one thing we were born searching for—a deep and intimate relationship with Him. Believe Him, trust that His heart is good, and follow Him with all your heart, soul, mind, and strength.

EMBRACING THE TRUTH - 20 MINUTES

LEADER INSTRUCTIONS FOR GROUP EXPERIENCE: *Show a scene from the movie Star Wars Episode VI: Return of the Jedi. The climactic scene occurs when Luke is finally able to pull his father, Anakin Skywalker become the evil Darth Vader, back from the "Dark Side." This clip is in scenes 43, 44, and part of 45. These scenes run from 1:55:02 to 1:57:43 minutes and 1:59:28-2:01:40 minutes on the DVD. (Queue up scene 43 before your session.)*

GIVE THIS BACKGROUND: *In this movie, Anakin had been seduced by the evil Emperor and the dark side of the Force, and he became the feared Darth Vader. He has vowed to win his son, Luke, to the dark side or destroy him. Luke continues to hold out hope that he can draw his father back to the light side. Luke battles Darth and stops him, but is now face-to-face with the evil emperor, refusing to join him on the dark side.*

PULLED FROM BOTH SIDES

1. What decision did Darth Vader (Anakin) face in this scene? What do you think finally rekindled the spirit of the Jedi in him, and turned him back to the light side? How can you relate to Vader in your own story?

2. Vader thought it was too late for him to turn from the bondage of the dark side. Why do you think he felt that way? Even though he was dying, Darth told Luke that he had "saved" him. What did he mean?

We discussed that resistance to change, especially major life change, can occur for many reasons. One that most of us struggle with is doubting the heart of God toward us. We believed the lies of the evil emperor in our story. But let's look at God's heart and plan.

17 For God did not send his Son into the world to condemn the world, but to save the world through him ... 21 But whoever lives by the truth comes into the light.

JOHN 3:17,20 NIV

For you have not received a spirit of slavery leading to fear again, but you have received a spirit of adoption as sons by which we cry out, "Abba [or Daddy]! Father!"

ROMANS 8:15 NASB

No eye has seen, no ear has heard, no mind has conceived what God has prepared for those who love Him.

1 CORINTHIANS 2:9 NIV

As Vader turned back to the light, not only was he saved from evil, but his entire life was redeemed. A wave of redemption was set in place – redemption for his son and daughter, for those battling with him, and ultimately for many oppressed by the dark side.

3. According to John 3:17 and Romans 8:15, what was God's reason for sending Jesus to die for you? What should be your attitude as you approach God to wrestle with Him?

4. Has God given you a fresh vision for your life (1 Corinthians 2:9)? How would you feel if God not only rescued you from your bondage, but then gave you a new future of and redeemed your past?

CONNECTING - 20 MINUTES

PREPARING FOR CHANGE

To be entirely ready for God to forgive, restore, and redeem us, we each have to settle three issues: (1) Accepting that God is really crazy about you personally; (2) Setting aside pride and putting yourself in God's hands, yet not let your "hands hang limp"; and (3) Placing your trust in God to lead you down the unfamiliar path to healing.

[God speaking to Israel ... and to us today:] ¹¹ *On that day you will not be put to shame for all the wrongs you have done to me, because I will remove from this city those who rejoice in their pride. Never again will you be haughty on my holy hill.* ¹² *But I will leave within you the meek and humble, who trust in the name of the LORD. ...* ¹⁵ *The LORD has taken away our punishment, he has turned back your enemy. The LORD, the King of Israel, is with you; never again will you fear any harm.* ¹⁶ *On that day they will say to Jerusalem, "Do not fear, O Zion; do not let your hands hang limp.* ¹⁷ *The LORD, your God is with you, he is mighty to save. He will take great delight in you, he will quiet you with his love, he will rejoice over you with singing."*

ZEPHANIAH 3:11-12,15-17 NIV

1. God promises that He won't put us to shame (verse 11) and will take away our punishment (verse 15). Why can that be hard for some of us to accept?

2. What does verse 17 tell you about God's heart toward you personally? How does it make you feel when you hear that God takes "great delight in you" and "rejoices over you with singing"?

3. How can we be humble enough to put ourselves in God's hands, and yet not let our "hands hang limp"? What might be some ways we can be engaged and active in God's process of forgiving, restoring, and redeeming us?

There's no magic formula or genie in a lamp to instantly zap our addictions away. Our behaviors, good or bad, come out of our thoughts, feelings, and ultimately, what we truly believe in our innermost being. Behavioral changes alone won't free us from an addiction for long, but radical heart surgery will. The Lord knows what we need, but open-heart surgery is always elective with God. It's up to each of us.

The process of changing hearts and redeeming lives doesn't fit the model of self-help books or the paths we've been down before. This path to healing is unfamiliar and probably even scary to some. It feels dangerous, risky, and insecure. And it's never the same for anybody.

[The Lord speaking about leading His people:] ¹⁶ I will lead the blind by ways they have not known, along unfamiliar paths I will guide them, I will turn darkness into light before them and make the rough places smooth. These are the things I will do; I will not forsake them. ¹⁷ But those who trust in idols, who say to images, "You are our gods," will be turned back in utter shame.

ISAIAH 42:16-17 NIV

4. In what ways do you feel "blind" as you take this recovery path? What's your deepest concern or fear about taking the unfamiliar path to healing (Isaiah 42:16)?

How can this group hold you up in prayer today and through this week? What practical, support, or accountability needs can this group help you with this week?

Go around the group with each of you praying for the person on your left.

MY PRAYER REQUESTS & NEEDS:

My Group's Prayer Requests & Needs:

Closing Recovery Prayer:

Dear God, we're baffled by the fact that You care so deeply about each and every one of us. On the one hand, we're excited about seeing how you plan to change us, but we're also scared to death about walking blindly down unfamiliar paths. Give each of us a genuine experience of Your presence this week.

Taking it Home

LEADER: *Strongly encourage everyone to continue their preparation process at home throughout the week, using the "My Story" questions and daily journaling. Most of all, create expectancy in group members about spending a period of time with God in order to hear from Him personally.*

NOTE: *Be sure that people who have not shared the full story of their addictions with at least one person make that a big priority this week. Offer to help as the listener or find someone who can.*

My Story: Trust in the Holy Spirit to open your eyes & heart as you write.

1. List some times when you've clearly felt God's presence in your life.

2. Which of the following areas do I struggle with most? Why do I struggle with this specifically?

- Accepting that God delights in me personally?

- Believing that God won't put me to shame like my "idols" or counterfeit lovers?

- Letting God control my path, and actively engaging in His agenda?

- Placing my trust in God to lead me down the unfamiliar path to healing?

3. How willing are you for God to reach out to you ... really?

QUESTIONS TO TAKE TO GOD:

Try to carve out an extended time to pour out your heart and listen to God.

When you ask God a question, expect His Spirit to respond to your heart and spirit. Be careful not to rush it or manufacture an answer. Don't write down what you think the "right answer" is. Don't turn the Bible into a reference book or spiritual encyclopedia. Just pose your question to God and wait on Him to answer. Focus on listening to God, and be sure to record what you hear and sense He is saying to you.

　　 ✳ God, do you really take "great delight" in me as Zephaniah says, or do You just tolerate me? What is it about me that makes You laugh, sing, and really enjoy me?

IDEAS FOR YOUR DAILY JOURNAL: (as simple as a spiral notebook)
- Times that I sense God's presence and His personal touches in my life
- Thoughts and feelings about God, other people, my life situation, and myself
- Lies I've been believing, about God, other people, my life situation, and myself
- Struggles and failures this week, and my response to them
- Times I'm living as a New Creation, embracing the God-given desires of my new heart (even small steps in this direction are huge!)

I believe I'm as ready as I'm going to be for Step 7. In Step 6 I've wrestled with God, and I trust Him to lead me along the unfamiliar path to healing and freedom. I have become entirely ready to have God forgive, restore, and redeem my life.

Signed_____ Date: _____

A CHANGE OF HEART AND MIND (STEP 7)

BREAKING THE ICE - 10 MINUTES

> **LEADER:** *Recovery from addictions is not an easy process. Use these "Breaking the Ice" to start things on a lighter note. This can be another time for group members to deepen relationships, but keep the tone upbeat and fun. Encourage each person to participate.*

1. Which of these vacation plans sounds the best to you and why?
   - ☐ The beach on the French Riviera
   - ☐ A cruise ship to anywhere
   - ☐ Hiking in the Rocky Mountains
   - ☐ Skiing in the Alps
   - ☐ I love New York ...
   - ☐ Salmon fishing in Alaska
   - ☐ Snorkeling in the Great Barrier Reef
   - ☐ Enjoying the exotic Far East
   - ☐ Touring through Europe
   - ☐ Chilling out in tropical Tahiti
   - ☐ Other: _____

2. When you were a child or young adult, what were some of the most outrageous things you "wanted to be when you grew up"?

3. How did your "Taking it Home" assignment go? What have you wrestled with God about? What has been the outcome so far?

4. Did God answer your question about what He enjoys about you? Were you surprised? Share with the group about your time with God.

Opening Prayer:

God, we are taking this unfamiliar path to recovery, healing, and freedom, but we often do feel blind. We desperately need You to lead us on. Each of us has his or her own unique path, but we take comfort in our Abba, or Loving Dad, taking every step with us. Help us to grasp the impact of the divinely powerful weapons we'll discuss in this session.

In Step 6: The path to recovery is unfamiliar and even scary at times. It doesn't follow conventional human wisdom or any self-help book. We discussed what it means to be a New Creation in Christ. We learned that God invites us to wrestle with Him over our pains and questions. He also wants us to bring our deepest questions and thirsts to him.

In Step 7: Each step in the process is vital, but in Step 7 we begin to open the door to healing and change. This step will make use of the work you did to map the DNA of your addictions. We will ask Jesus to correct our wrong beliefs, and change us from the inside out. As we invite Father, Son, and Holy Spirit into our hearts and minds, we will see change ... and that's exciting!

Objectives for this Step:

- Broaden our view of the Father's heart and gifts He gives us
- Internalize the truth that God loves us and wants the best for us
- Recognize the power in God's mercy and forgiveness that's available to each of us
- Grasp how God changes us from the inside out
- Commit to spending extended times with God for restoration and repentance

Discovering the Truth - 35 minutes

LEADER: *Ask various group members to read explanations and Bible passages throughout this section. The initial part of "Discovering the Truth," focuses on God's care for us. Then you'll unwrap the divinely powerful weapons of forgiveness and new life. Leave time for the "Embracing the Truth" and "Connecting" segments.*

Step 7 is the first step toward seeking healing and change in our Recovery Map: ASK GOD TO BEGIN TO RESTORE & REDEEM YOUR LIFE: We humbly ask Jesus to correct our wrong beliefs, and to change our lives from the inside out.

RECOVERY MAP

STARTING WITH	1	1. Admit your need
DECISION	2	2. Find new power
	3	3. Make a decision
SEARCHING	4	4. Take inventory
MY SELF	5	5. Admit your addiction to others
	6	6. Prepare for change
SEEKING HEALING	**7**	**7. Ask God to restore & redeem life**
& CHANGE	8	8. Identify resentments & offenses
	9	9. Make amends
STICKING	10	10. Be preventative
WITH IT	11	11. Stay connected with God
	12	12. Share your story

Change is always difficult for anybody, but when we look back recovered, restored, and redeemed, we'll know without a doubt that any difficulties were worth it.

MORE THAN YOU CAN IMAGINE

If each of us could truly understand God's heart for us and the incredible life He wants for us, then our resistance would fade away. The villain in the story doesn't want that to happen. He knows the truth will set you free from his bonds of lies and distortions.

[David's prayer in a time of fear:] ⁸ You have taken account of my wanderings; put my tears in Your bottle. Are they not in Your book? ... ¹¹ In God have I put my trust, I shall not be afraid. What can man do to me? ¹² Your vows are binding upon me , O God; I will render thank offerings to You. ¹³ for You have delivered my soul from death, indeed my feet from stumbling, so that I may walk before God in the light of the living.

PSALM 56:8,11-13 NASB

[16] I pray that out of his glorious riches he may strengthen you with power through his Spirit in your inner being. [17] so that Christ may dwell in your hearts through faith. And I pray that you, being rooted and established in love, [18] may have power, altogether with the saints, to grasp how long and high and wide and deep is the love of Christ, [19] and to know this love that surpasses knowledge—that you may be filled to the measure of all the fullness of God. [20] Now to him who is able to do immeasurably more than all we can ask of imagine, according to his power that is at work in us ...

EPHESIANS 3:16-20 NIV

1. According to Psalm 56:8, how much interest does God take in each individual life? How does it make you feel that He collects every one of your tears in a bottle and tracks your "wanderings" and hurts in His daily diary?

2. What supernatural assets and resources does God have that He's anxious to give us, His children, if we will fully trust and follow Him?

   - Psalm 56:12 –

   - Psalm 56:13 –

   - Ephesians 3:16 –

   - Ephesians 3:17 –

   - Ephesians 3:19 –

   - Ephesians 3:20 –

NO SHAME, ALL GAIN

We carry so much shame from our destruction choices and behaviors. Going to the holy God with our shameful thoughts and actions is the last thing most of want to do. But let's see how God approaches our shame.

[3] We too were once foolish, disobedient, deceived, captives of various passions and pleasures, living in malice and envy, hateful, detesting one another. [4] But when the goodness and love for man appeared from God our Savior, [5] He saved us—not by works of righteousness that we had done, but according to His mercy, through the washing of regeneration and renewal by the Holy Spirit. [6] This [Spirit] He poured out on us abundantly through Jesus Christ our Savior, [7] so that having been justified by his grace, we may become heirs with the hope of eternal life.

TITUS 3:3-7 HCSB

¹ No condemnation now exists for those in Christ Jesus, ² because the Spirit's law of life in Christ Jesus has set you free from the law of sin and death ... ¹¹ And if the Spirit of Him who raised Jesus from the dead lives in you, then He who raised Christ from the dead will also bring your mortal bodies to life through his Spirit who lives in you.

ROMANS 8:1-2,11 HCSB

¹⁰ With the heart one believes, resulting in righteousness, and with the mouth one confesses, resulting in salvation. ¹¹ Now the Scripture says, "No one who believes on Him will be put to shame" ... ¹³ For everyone who calls on the name of the Lord will be saved.

ROMANS 10:10-11,13 HCSB

3. What specific causes, both inside and outside of our hearts, does God focus on for sins and destructive behaviors (Titus 3:3)?

4. According to Romans 8:1 and 10:11, how does God approach shame? Do you think shame and condemnation are something He wants His children to have? Explain.

5. What amazing privileges does Jesus impart to us (Titus 3:7; Romans 8:1; 10:13)? What privileges does the Holy Spirit bring to us (Titus 3:5,7; Romans 8:2,11)?

DIVINELY POWERFUL WEAPON: FORGIVENESS

God never wanted us to feel shame and condemnation. He wants our guilt to drive us to seek Him so that we can get back on track. The word "devil" means "accuser." It's the Devil who condemns and works to keep us from God's restoration.

⁴ For day and night your hand was heavy upon me; my strength was sapped as in the heat of summer. ⁵ Then I acknowledged my sin to you and did not cover up my iniquity. I said, "I will confess my transgressions to the LORD"—and you forgave the guilt of my sin.

PSALM 32: 4-5 NIV

¹ *Be gracious to me, O God, according to Your lovingkindness; according to the greatness of Your compassion blot out my transgressions. ...* ⁶ *Behold, You desire truth in the innermost being, and in the hidden part You will make me know wisdom.* ⁷ *Purify me with hysssop, and I shall be clean; Wash me, and I shall be whiter than snow.* ⁸ *Make me hear joy and gladness. Let the bones which You have broken rejoice.* ⁹ *Hide Your face from my sins and blot out all my iniquities.* ¹⁰ *Create in me a clean heart, O God, and renew a steadfast spirit within me.* ¹² *Restore to me the joy of Your salvation and sustain me with a willing spirit.*

PSALM 51:1,6-10,12 NASB

6. God loves us so much. What does He do when unresolved guilt and shame are festering in our hearts (Psalm 32:4 and Psalm 51:6)?

7. With what attitude do you hear David, the psalmist, approaching God (Psalm 32:5 and Psalm 51:1,8)? What attitude and action is required on our part to open ourselves to God's forgiveness (Psalm 32:5 and Psalm 51:10,12)?

8. According to Psalms 32 and 51, what are some of the benefits that result from our humble confession of sins or failures, and God's compassionate forgiveness?

Romans 10:10 highlighted the power of what we believe and the power of what we speak out to confess. When we humbly go to God and confess our failures and sins, He promises to forgive us every time (1 John 1:9) ... amazing! Ephesians 3:16 and Psalm 51:6 show us that the Spirit teaches us in the "hidden part," so we change from the inside out.

EMBRACING THE TRUTH - 20 MINUTES

LEADER: *This "Embracing the Truth" will help group members begin to integrate the truths about confession, forgiveness, and repentance into their lives. The goal is to change our thinking about repentance and realize that it's a powerful tool that needs to be used every single day in our lives. Again, ask volunteers to read the Bible readings aloud for the group.*

DIVINELY POWERFUL WEAPON: REPENTANCE

God's forgiveness, with our confession, is a very powerful weapon in our lives, but it's not enough. We also need repentance. Unfortunately, that word has been given a bad connotation over the years. Most people immediately think about hellfire preaching, you know — "Repent or your achin' bacon is going to be deep fried in the bonfires of hell."

Actually, "repent" comes for the Greek word *metanoia*, which means to change (*meta*) our mind-set or understanding (*noia*). The word "metamorphosis" is a related term, meaning a change in form or substance, and is used to describe what occurs when a caterpillar retreats into it's cocoon to emerge as a butterfly.

¹ As we have received mercy, we do not give up. ² Instead, we have renounced the shameful, secret things, not walking in deceit or distorting God's message, but in God's sight we commend ourselves to every person's conscience by an open display of the truth. ... ⁶ For God who said, "Light shall shine out of darkness"—He has shone in our hearts to give the light of the knowledge of God's glory in the face of Jesus Christ.

2 CORINTHIANS 4:1-2,6 HCSB

¹ I urge you, brothers, in view of God's mercy, to offer your bodies as living sacrifices, holy and pleasing to God —this is your spiritual act of worship. ² Do not conform any longer to the pattern of this world, but be transformed by the renewing of your mind. Then you will be able to test and approve what God's will is —His good, pleasing, and perfect will.

ROMANS 12:1-2 NIV

1. According to 2 Corinthians 4:2 what are the four things that we need to renounce and ask God to transform (change in our understanding)? What's the prescribed antidote in verses 2 and 6?

2. In Romans 12:1, "brothers" refers to believers or Christ-followers. What two decisions do we need to make in order to allow God to renew our minds and transform us (verses 1 and 2)?

As we turn to God and renounce our secrets, our shame, our false beliefs, and our distorted perspectives, we unleash even more divinely powerful weapons. Some of these weapons are revealed to us; others are mysterious and occur in the spiritual realm.

4 The weapons we fight with are not the weapons of the world. On the contrary, they have divine power to demolish strongholds. 5 We demolish arguments and every pretension that sets itself up against the knowledge of God, and we take captive every thought to make it obedient to Christ.

2 CORINTHIANS 10:4-5 NIV

3. Where is the cosmic battle between good and evil being waged according to 2 Corinthians 10:5? What are the "strongholds" we must demolish in this battle?

As we recognize the battle being waged over our minds and hearts, it becomes clearer why change must occur from the inside out, beginning in our innermost being—our hearts and minds. So we're back again to our "Captive Heart Model." Our part in repentance is to persistently decide to turn or return to God.

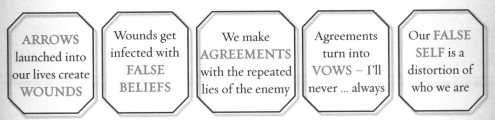

| ARROWS launched into our lives create WOUNDS | Wounds get infected with FALSE BELIEFS | We make AGREEMENTS with the repeated lies of the enemy | Agreements turn into VOWS – I'll never ... always | Our FALSE SELF is a distortion of who we are |

* Captive Heart Model & Critical Path to Healing developed by Ron Keck.

4. The Holy Spirit can transform you, renew your mind with God's truth, and help you take every thought captive to make it obedient to Jesus. In what ways would you expect to experience transformation in the five areas of the "Captive Heart Model?"

• Your Wounds –

• False Beliefs –

• Agreements I've Made –

• Vows I've Taken –

• My Distorted False Self –

17 Now the Lord is the Spirit, and where the Spirit of the Lord is, there is freedom. 18 And we who with unveiled faces all reflect the Lord's glory, are being transformed into his likeness with ever-increasing glory, which comes from the Lord, who is the Spirit.

2 CORINTHIANS 3:17-18 NIV

5. According to 2 Corinthians 3:18, what's the purpose of this ongoing, continual transformation—change from the inside out?

CONNECTING - 25 MINUTES

TRANSFORMED ...

The unfamiliar paths and weapons you'll encounter in your life of repentance will affect every area of your life. Remember, every behavior is linked to an underlying belief. When you repent, you turn away from your old, destructive ways, and turn toward the new, constructive ways of truth and light. In this way God restores and then redeems your life.

[10] *Distress that drives us to God ... turns us around. It gets us back in the way of salvation. We never regret that kind of pain. But those who let distress drive them away from God are full of regrets, and end up on a deathbed of regrets.* [11] *And now, isn't it wonderful all the ways in which this distress has goaded you closer to God? You're more alive, more concerned, more sensitive, more reverent, more human, more passionate, more responsible. Looked at from this angle, you've come out of this with purity of heart.*

2 CORINTHIANS 7:10-11 MESSAGE

[19] *Repent and return, so that your sins may be wiped away, in order that times of refreshing may come from the presence of the Lord;* [20] *and that He may send Jesus, the Christ appointed for you.*

ACTS 3:19-20 NASB

1. As your distress drives you to God, which of God's rewards of repentance in 2 Corinthians 7:10-11 and Acts 3:19-20 are you most looking forward to and why?

LEADER INSTRUCTIONS FOR THE GROUP EXPERIENCE: *This group experience provides a dramatic demonstration of our confession and God's forgiveness.*

> *SUPPLIES: A tub or bucket filled with water; Dissolvo® paper from a magic supply house or Web site; markers to write on the Dissolvo® paper*
>
> *PROCEDURE: Give each person a slip of Dissolvo® paper. Lead the group through the prayer exercise below. After the prayer exercise, invite group members to come and toss their papers into the water and watch the results.*
>
> *SOME WEB SOURCES:*
> - *www.gospelmagic.com*
> - *www.ronjo.com*
> - *www.dissolvo.com (look under creative products)*

We've been reminded that if we confess our sins, wounds, false beliefs to God, and failures. He'll forgive, renew, transform, restore, redeem. Let's take some time to begin doing Step 7 now in a "Listening Prayer" exercise.

LISTENING PRAYER TIME:

You're going to lead group members in a short time of listening prayer.
- *Allow this experience some time; don't rush it.*
- *Put on quiet background music (use the CD Pursued by God: Redemptive Worship Volume 1 from Serendipity House, or select your own music); dim the lights if possible.*
- *Help each person create a small personal area. This is not a time to chat; make it very honoring.*
- *Trust God to speak to each person individually.*

DIRECTIONS ... Ask group members these questions:

1. Ask God to show you how He feels about your pain, your failures, and your addictions.

2. Now ask Him how He feels about you.

3. Invite God to bring to mind the wound, failure, sin, or wrong thinking that He wants you to confess right now so that He can forgive you, free you from it's grip, and begin to restore you.

4. Humbly confess that issue or false belief to God and ask for the forgiveness He promises.

5. Accept God's mercy and forgiveness ... allow that burden of guilt and shame to lift off of you.

Following the "Listening Prayer Time," take out the special slip of paper your leader gave you. With a marker or pen, write down the issue, failure, sin, or false belief that you confessed to God. Fold the slip of paper and take it to the front of the room as your leader instructs.

2. What did you hear from God during this experience? What feelings did you have as you saw the thing you confessed disintegrate before your eyes?

As you spend time with God allowing Him to forgive, restore, and redeem you, those will be amazing times of godly sorrow followed by release and freedom. The enemy will continue to feed lies to us about God's goodness to try to force us into despair. His goal is to isolate, enslave, and destroy us. But working through this process with Father, Son, and Spirit will lead you down unfamiliar paths toward a great end, which the prophet Isaiah wrote about as Jesus' mission and life passion.

The Spirit of the Sovereign LORD is upon me to preach good news to the poor. He sent me to bind up the brokenhearted, to proclaim freedom for the captives and release from darkness for the prisoners, to proclaim the year of the LORD's favor and the day of vengeance of our God, to comfort all who mourn, to provide for those who grieve in Zion—to bestow on them the crown of beauty instead of ashes, the oil of gladness instead of mourning, and a garment of praise instead of a spirit of despair.

ISAIAH 61:1-3 NIV

3. What hope and promise did you hear in these words? Which words in Isaiah 61:1-3 give you new hope as you begin to grasp that Jesus really cares about you personally, and that He also wants to replace beauty for ashes, praise for despair, light for darkness, and freedom for addiction?

LEADER PRAYER OPTION: *Page 4 shows a music CD:* Pursued by God: Redemptive Worship Volume 1 *from Serendipity House. In place of your group prayer time, you may want to playing the song "Wash Me" from that CD. Download lyrics from www.SerendipityHouse.com/Community (under Group Leaders - Practical Tools). Ask group members to close their eyes and listen, and then at the end of the song privately respond back to God.*

MY PRAYER REQUESTS & NEEDS:

MY GROUP'S PRAYER REQUESTS & NEEDS:

CLOSING RECOVERY PRAYER:

Holy Spirit, thanks for joining us today. Thanks too for Your mercy and love that has made a way for us to release our guilt and shame, our struggles and wounds. What a gift forgiveness is! Please help each of us this week to set aside the blocks of time we need to spend with you in repentance, restoration, and redemption.

GROUP PROGRESS CHECK

Step 7 in our recovery is the central and most vital step. It cannot and should NOT be rushed. Depending upon the amount of redemptive work each person has to do with God, this step could take an extra week or two. Give people time, but poll group members when you next meet, and when the majority of your group is ready, move ahead to Step 8.

... You'll very likely need to CONTINUE the Session 8 "PRAYER EXPERIENCE" through the bulk of your next meeting. Before diving into that though, spend a little time catching up. Be sure to celebrate any victories that your group members are experiencing.

TAKING IT HOME

LEADER: *Strongly encourage group members to carry a notebook and Bible into their extended times with God. Emphasize that Step 7 is never just a quick prayer time. It requires extended times of pouring out our hearts and listening to God. Discourage procrastination so this pivotal step becomes a priority. This is a great time for accountability partners to join together and support each other.*

Healing and Change Begin ...

Steps 7-9 will be not be a one-time deal. We'll need to be continually sensitive as the Holy Spirit reveals other character defects, sins, false beliefs, and our emerging false self. The best path to "ever-increasing glory" is to develop a lifestyle of taking the unfamiliar path with God. BUT ... this first one-time deal will be crucial for you to break through the wall, and begin to experience forgiveness, freedom, restoration, and redemption.

What You'll Need:

(1) Trust that God will show up, listen, and speak to you
(2) Notebook or paper and a pen to capture what God reveals and your feelings
(3) Your journal that includes your mapping of the DNA of your addiction
(4) Have a Bible on hand
(5) If possible, the person that you shared the details of your addiction with in Step 5

Ask God to forgive, renew, restore, redeem ...

You will definitely want to refer to your journal, as well as your addictions DNA map, and notes and Scriptures you've highlighted in this book. But, even more so, be open and sensitive to the leading of the Spirit. For God, there is no darkness, no unfamiliar path, no distortion, no deception. He knows the way out for you!

Be sure to discuss each of these areas with God during your times, allowing Him to reveal strongholds in your life ... areas you need to confess ... deep issues that require repentance and renewal ... places where you desperately need restoration and redemption.

AREAS TO DISCUSS WITH GOD:

- My Wounds & Resentments

- Your Guilt & Shame

- My Counterfeit Lovers that Have Pulled Your Affections from God

- Lies or False Beliefs

- Faulty Agreements I've Made & Vows I've Taken

- Emergence of My Distorted False Self

- Passions and Desires Distorted from God-given Passions

- Your Ruts and Well-Worn Patterns of Behavior

BE SURE TO KEEP A JOURNAL of the changes in your relationship with God, along with the heart and life transformations you experience.

SESSION 8

IN HARM'S WAY (STEP 8)

BREAKING THE ICE - 15 MINUTES

GROUP PROGRESS CHECK

Step 7 in our recovery was the central and most vital step. It cannot and should NOT be rushed. Depending upon the amount of redemptive work each person has to do with God, this step could take an extra week or two. Give people time, but poll group members when you next meet, and when the majority of your group is ready, move ahead to Step 8.

... You'll very likely need to CONTINUE the Session 7 "LISTENING PRAYER TIME" before continuing on with Session 8.. Before diving into prayer, spend a little time catching up. Be sure to celebrate any victories that your group members are experiencing.

INSTRUCTIONS FOR GROUP EXPERIENCE: *Following initial greetings and welcome, read the paragraph that follows, and show a clip from the movie* Meet the Parents. *In this scene, offenses are flying everywhere in the game of water volleyball. Show the first half of scene 12 that runs from 59:00 to 1:01:18 minutes on the DVD.*

In the movie *Meet the Parents*, male nurse Greg Focker (played by Ben Stiller) is poised to propose to his girlfriend Pam (Teri Polo), but he must first get the approval of her hard-nosed father Jack (Robert De Niro). Greg and Jack mix like oil and water, but Greg is doing everything he can to impress Pam's family and friends.

1. What do you think blonde, athletic Kevin's motivation was in giving Greg playing tips? What do you think motivated girlfriend Pam's comments, and the remarks from Greg's teammates? What other hurtful speech and behaviors did you notice?

2. Who did Greg end up offending? What was his intent? He realized his offense, but why do you think nobody else realized they'd offended him?

3. Some call particular personal annoyances, "pet peeves." Identify one of your pet peeves.
   - ☐ People driving while talking on cell phones, putting on make-up, or shaving
   - ☐ Endless e-mail forwards on the computer
   - ☐ The incessant yapping of the neighbor's dog
   - ☐ A brand new car that keeps breaking down
   - ☐ A beautiful but crying baby behind you on an airplane
   - ☐ Someone smacking their mouth while eating
   - ☐ Inconsiderate people behind the wheel, or in the checkout line at a store
   - ☐ Other: _____

4. How is your healing and restoration work with God going? Would you like to share any meaningful point of reconnection with God, of repentance, or of restoration?

OPENING PRAYER:

God, there's no way to tell You how grateful we are for Your love, forgiveness, and restoration. As we continue on, we're still dependent on You. When we're stuck and life is dragging us down, it's easy to become self-centered—absorbed with our own issues, and oblivious to the damage we're leaving in our wake as we speed through life. Help us to lift our heads and see others with Your eyes.

IN STEP 7: We began to open the door to healing and change from the inside out as we took our wounds and resentments, guilt and shame, false beliefs and distorted passions to God and exchanged them for forgiveness, transformation, restoration, and redemption.

IN STEP 8: As we continue to focus on our own healing with God, we also need now to lift our heads and take steps to heal and restore relationships with other people. To take this step, we must come to grips with our offenses and our resentments. Until we address these relational issues, we cannot be fully free.

OBJECTIVES FOR THIS STEP:

- Understand the limitations of being human and the cycle of pain that results
- Define who we've hurt and the nature of the hurt, and then determine to make amends
- Accept that forgiveness is a process that takes time and must come from the heart

DISCOVERING THE TRUTH - 35 MINUTES

> **LEADER:** *Invite group members to read various explanations and Bible passages. "Discovering the Truth" helps group members recognize the damage their addictions and self-focus have caused. Much of the discussion focuses on the divinely powerful weapons of forgiveness between people.*

Step 8 is the next step toward seeking healing and change: IDENTIFY MY RESENTMENTS AND OFFENSES: We make a list of all the people we've harmed, and those who have harmed us. Then, we determine to forgive and make amends to them all.

RECOVERY MAP

STARTING WITH	I	1. Admit your need
DECISION	2	2. Find new power
	3	3. Make a decision
SEARCHING	4	4. Take inventory
MY SELF	5	5. Admit your addiction to others
	6	6. Prepare for change
SEEKING HEALING	7	7. Ask God to restore & redeem life
& CHANGE	**8**	**8. Identify resentments & offenses**
	9	9. Make amends
STICKING	10	10. Be preventative
WITH IT	11	11. Stay connected with God
	12	12. Share your story

THE HARD STUFF OF RELATIONSHIPS

The consensus of people that have gone through the 12 Steps is that steps 8-9 are both the most difficult and most healing. Our inclination is to let the past stay in the past, and move on with life. And yet, without dealing with our resentments and accepting responsibility for what we have done, it's difficult to move on to the future.

13 As a father has compassion on his children, so the LORD has compassion on those who fear Him. 14 For He knows what we are made of, remembering that we are dust.   PSALM 103:13-14 HCSB

10 Now I plead with you, brethren, by the name of our Lord Jesus Christ, that you all speak the same thing, and that there be no divisions among you, but that you be perfectly joined together in the same mind and in the same judgment. 11 For it has been declared to me concerning you, my brethren, by those of Chloe's household, that there are contentions among you.

PISTE 1 CORINTHIANS 1:10-11 NKJV

1 How good and pleasant it is for when brothers live together in unity! 2 It is like precious oil poured on the head, running down on the beard ... 3 For there the LORD bestows his blessing, even life forevermore.

PSALM 133:1-3 NIV

1. In Psalm 103:14, God recognizes our material of origin – dust (Genesis 1). Why does He does He do this? What is the point He's highlighting?

2. Why do you think relational disharmony is so common, even amongst people within the church?

3. Why does Psalm 133 make such a big deal about unity and harmony between people? Why is Paul pleading with the people in 1 Corinthians 1:10?

None of us is perfect ... except God. We have an enemy stirring up strife in our relationships, and we're all dealing with life the best we know how. God doesn't expect perfection from "dust." We also would do well to allow each other to be human. Most of the time, we cut ourselves more slack than we give others.

RESPONDING TO OFFENSES & RESENTMENTS

Healthy relationships are vital to a thriving, happy life. Past difficulties damage our relationships. Thinking about who we've harmed as a result of our addiction and self-focus ... who has hurt us ... and how we restore relationships are all important to our recovery. Recovery is proven by the way we live in relationship with people we know and love ... and even those who don't like us much.

12 So, as those who have been chosen of God, holy and beloved, put on the heart of compassion, kindness, humility, gentleness and patience; 13 bearing with one another, and forgiving each other, whoever has a complaint against anyone; just as the Lord forgave you, so also should you [forgive each other]. 14 Beyond all these things put on love, which is the perfect bond of unity. 15 Let the peace of Christ rule in your hearts, to which indeed you were called in one body; and be thankful.

COLOSSIANS 3:12-15 NASB

4. What do you see as the difference between "bearing with" and "forgiving" each other (Colossians 3:13)? Which comes more naturally to you?

5. What are some offenses where "bearing with one another" is called for? What kind of offenses require "intentional" forgiveness?

6. "Just as the Lord forgave you" – What do you think the point of this is? What are the full implications of this in the way you respond to people who have hurt you? How about the your relationship with God?

Forbearance and forgiveness form a nicely balanced pair of responses to two kinds of offenses. We should "bear with" or overlook *annoyances and unintentional* offenses. The offender didn't mean to hurt us, and often didn't even know he or she did. The difficult work of forgiveness is required for *intentional and deeper* offenses, when someone either deliberately hurts us or the offense go deep. These create resentment because we feel assaulted, betrayed, or unfairly treated. Forgiveness is not natural; it's a divinely powerful weapon that we can use only because the Lord forgave us.

When It's Hard to Forgive

True forgiveness is seldom easy, and it can be quite costly, but it's a powerful weapon for tearing down the strongholds in our innermost being. When we forgive, release, and help others, we are blessed and healed in the process.

7. What types of offenses do you find difficult to forgive? Do you think we should forgive no matter how we feel and even if our heart is not in it?

Embracing the Truth - 25 minutes

LEADER: *We've looked at the natural issues that occur in relationships and focused on responding to offense and resentments. Jesus sets the standard for forgiveness in His teaching and action. Let's personalize the truths we've seen. Let's learn to ask ourselves how Jesus would treat the people with whom we struggle.*

How to Forgive

We'll need to ask the Spirit to help us forgive others in the same way Jesus forgives us:

- We should acknowledge our pain and woundedness rather than pretending the hurt or betrayal didn't matter.
- We recognize that people hurt others out of their own woundedness, so we lovingly, but firmly, confront our offender about the pain he or she has caused.
- We separate the person from his or her offense, and we choose to forgive, canceling that person's debt and punishment. You choose not to get even.

[8] Live in harmony with one another; be sympathetic, love as brothers, be compassionate and humble. [9] Do not repay evil for evil or insult for insult, but with blessing, because to this you were called so that you may inherit a blessing.

1 Peter 3:8-9 NIV

Above all, keep your love for one another at full strength, since love covers a multitude of sins.

1 Peter 4:8 HCSB

See to it that no one misses the grace of God and that no bitter root grows up to cause trouble and defile many.

HEBREWS 12:15 NIV

1. Because they're human, people will tick us off, hurt us, and even betray us at times. According to 1 Peter 3:9 and 4:8, why is it so important for us to choose the way of forgiveness?

2. According to Hebrews 12:15, What will happen when we don't forgive from our hearts? What if our forgiveness is premature – before we've dealt with our hurt or anger? How about if it's not from our hearts, and superficial?

3. What are some key perspectives, listed in 1 Peter 3:8-9 and 4:8, that we need to ask God to instill in us so that He enables us to forgive and walk through a healthy forgiveness process?

[25] Laying aside falsehood, speak the truth each of you with his neighbor, for we are all members of one another. [26] Be angry, and yet do not sin

EPHESIANS 4:25-26 NASB

We discussed in an earlier session that the Greek word for "falsehood" (Ephesians 4:25) used in the original language of the New Testament literally refers to the masks that were worn in Greek theatre.

4. Is feeling or expressing anger always sinful and destructive. Explain.

[12] Be in agreement with one another. Do not be proud ... Do not be wise in your own estimation. [17] Do not repay anyone evil for evil. Try to do what is honorable in everyone's eyes. [18] If possible, on your part, live at peace with everyone. [19] Friends, do not avenge yourselves; instead, leave room for His wrath. For it is written: "Vengeance belongs to Me; I will repay," says the Lord.

ROMANS 12:16-19 HCSB

5. A destructive cycle begins when hurt people and they in turn hurt us, or when they seriously wound us and we retaliate. How do we break out of this destructive cycle (Romans 12:16-19)?

6. What does it mean to "leave room for God's wrath"? Why do you think God is so possessive and emphatic about vengeance belonging to Him (Romans 12:19)?

This forgiveness process takes TIME, but once we've allowed ourselves to truly feel anger, sadness, and hurt, then the next step is to begin to move toward forgiveness. As we do that, we take our offender off our hook and put him or her on God's hook. God is far more protective of us than we are, and He's far more qualified to avenge our hurts. As we release the desire for revenge, we can live in freedom, love, and hope. In forgiveness, we prevent a root of bitterness from destroying our hearts, joy, relationships, and recovery.

CONNECTING - 15 MINUTES

LEADER: *It's time to turn our attention from our resentments to the hurt we've caused in other people's lives in this "Connecting" time. Be sensitive to the feelings of group members as they share in this time together. Help people who are struggling to envision the benefits at the other end of the path they walk by faith in God.*

THE OTHER SIDE OF THE COIN

We've focused through most of this session on responding to offenses and dealing with our resentments. The flipside of that coin—identifying those people that we have harmed through our addictions and self-focus—also needs attention.

1. What are some ways we can hurt people, especially people that we care about? Brainstorm together as a group a list of ways any of us might have caused harm or loss to others through our addictions, destructive choices, operating out of our own woundedness, and so on.

2. Think about three broken or unreconciled relationships in your life. How ready are you to make amends to these people? Circle a rating number and explain.

1	2	3	4	5	6	7	8	9	10

I'm not ready
to make any
moves yet

I'm willing, but there are
still some personal issues
I need to work through

I'm ready to do
whatever it takes to
make amends with
this person

(If you're not ready to go out and make amends with everyone in your world, that's normal. The list is a tool to get you started thinking in that direction and making amends one at a time.)

3. It's time to share your burden again and allow the group to help you carry it. Which person on your list will be the most difficult to deal with? What do you think is the worst thing that could happen if you try to make amends?

Thinking of others and the wounds we've inflicted can be painful for us. Ignoring these relational issues, however, only makes matters worse. They stay below the surface and decay, resulting in bitterness taking root.

Exposing the secret and shameful things we've done breaks the power of secrecy and shame. Remember too that you're not in this alone. God's not shocked by what we've done (Psalm 103), and our group is cheering you on.

How can we help support you practically and specifically this week as you continue to think about and compile your list? We're ready to pray for you; what would your specific request be?

MY PRAYER REQUESTS & NEEDS:

MY GROUP'S PRAYER REQUESTS & NEEDS:

CLOSING RECOVERY PRAYER:
God, it's time to break the cycle of pain; to face some ugly things about ourselves and other wounded people that have hurt us. Walk with each one of us as we take the unfamiliar path through Step 8 this week. Enable us to forgive others as You have forgiven us.

TAKING IT HOME

LEADER: *"Taking it Home" this week is focused on helping group members to begin to work through two things: (1) beginning the process of forgiving people on their "Resentments List," and (2) creating a list of people they have a offended or hurt. Accountability partners should encourage each other.*

RESENTMENTS LIST:

1. Ask God to bring to your mind the people you've not let off the hook for things they've done to you. Make a list.

2. Note the person's offenses and your resentments next to each name.

3. Allow yourself to feel the hurt and anger over these offenses (this may take weeks).

4. Release the person who hurt you, and choose not to get even.

5. Identify obstacles to forgiving and releasing any of these people, and ask God to remove these obstacles.

AMENDS LIST:

1. Next, ask God to reveal to you people with whom you need to make amends (seek forgiveness and/or make restitution). Make that list.

2. Note your specific offenses toward each person on your list..

3. Allow yourself to feel the pain or loss you've caused each person (this may take weeks).

4. Prioritize your list with God, and determine what you need to say and do to make amends. Also, ask God to make you willing to do what it takes to make amends.

NOTES:

Sometimes, forgiveness can be instant. Sometimes, it requires fighting through a tough process. Stick with it! Fight with God until you're free!

There may be overlaps on your resentments and amends lists. In these cases, you'll need to work through forgiving these people before you're sincerely ready to make amends.

OPTIONAL IDEAS FOR YOUR DAILY JOURNAL:
- Emotions that surfaced as I've made my list
- Transformations God is making in my heart and mind
- Victories and progress I'm seeing in living as a New Creation in Christ
- Struggles and temporary setbacks

I still have steps to take, but I've made my list, spent time with God and my heart, begun the forgiveness process, and I'm ready to begin making amends with some priority person.

I've made a list of all the people I've harmed, and determined to make amends to them all.

Signed _____ Date: _____

GETTING BEYOND REGRETS (STEP 9)

BREAKING THE ICE - 10 MINUTES

> **LEADER:** *This "Breaking the Ice" time will help group members think about risks in life. They say the top three fears are speaking in public, heights, and snakes. This leads into later helping them explore risks they need to take in relationships. This may include a serious fear of rejection. Choose only 2 of the first 3 icebreakers that work for your group to keep things moving.*

1. They say the top three fears are speaking in public, heights, and snakes.
   Which of the following have the highest "Risk Factor" for you? Explain why.
   - ☐ Walking across a board several hundred feet up in the air
   - ☐ Speaking to an audience of 200 people for 20 minutes
   - ☐ Handling snakes and spiders for a natural history museum
   - ☐ Swimming with sharks for a documentary
   - ☐ Being replaced at work by a machine
   - ☐ Losing someone I really care about because of my behavior
   - ☐ Other: _____

2. What's the most valuable thing you've ever broken? What did that cost you?

3. What is the biggest "relationship risk" you've ever taken? What happened?

4. How did making your resentments and amends go? What was the hardest part of this for you? Were there any surprises for you in making your lists?

OPENING PRAYER:

God, this open-heart surgery that You're doing on us is painful, but we continue to follow You on these unfamiliar paths. We trust Your heart toward us, and know You want to set us free. Our lives have been filled with hurts. As hurt people, we have hurt other people. Help us to release those who have hurt us and make amends for the damage we've done.

IN STEP 8: We started taking steps to heal and restore relationships with other people. To take this step, we discussed our human limitations and flaws, and the way of forgiveness. Differentiating when to bear with someone and when forgiveness is required, we learned how to forgive. We also began the process of listing the people that we've hurt.

IN STEP 9: As we continue to focus on relationship mending, we will take the list of our offenses and resentments, and begin to act on it. Now that we've experienced God's forgiveness, we can forgive others and ask others to release us too. This will not and should always be easy; we'll discuss how to treat the responses of others.

OBJECTIVES FOR THIS STEP:

- Accept our responsibility for the hurt we've caused to others
- Learn how to make amends the way Jesus teaches us
- Replace some incorrect thinking about relationships with truth
- Understand drivers for bad responses, and ways to deal with them

DISCOVERING THE TRUTH - 35 MINUTES

> **LEADER:** *Invite group members to read various explanations and Bible passages. "Discovering the Truth" helps group members accept responsibility for the harm they have caused. The discussion will transition to the topic of how to make amends Jesus' way.*

Step 9 puts into action the work of Step 8: MAKE AMENDS: We make direct amends to people we've harmed whenever possible, except when to do so would injure them or others.

RECOVERY MAP

STARTING WITH DECISION	1	1. Admit your need
	2	2. Find new power
	3	3. Make a decision
SEARCHING MY SELF	4	4. Take inventory
	5	5. Admit your addiction to others
	6	6. Prepare for change
SEEKING HEALING & CHANGE	7	7. Ask God to restore & redeem life
	8	8. Identify resentments & offenses
	9	**9. Make amends**
STICKING WITH IT	10	10. Be preventative
	11	11. Stay connected with God
	12	12. Share your story

MIRACLES OF FORGIVENESS

Something amazing happens when we're finally able forgive people who have wounded us. Also, when we seek to make peace with those we've hurt, we give them opportunity to choose forgiveness and release. Whatever their response, we're released when we genuinely do our best. Don't minimize or underestimate this process. What seems a comparatively small offense or amend may actually be a life-altering event for the other person.

We've made our list and worked through some issues and resentments with God. There are three steps in the miracle of forgiveness and they must be taken.

1. Ask for and receive God's forgiveness. This was part of Step 7.

2. Forgive the person if he or she has hurt, abused, betrayed, or neglected us. We covered this in Step 8, and it's important to begin the process of working through our own hurts, especially in cases in which the same person in on both the resentments and amends lists.

3. Seek forgiveness and make amends to the person we've offended or hurt. Now that we've experienced God's forgiveness, we can ask others to release us as well. It's a BIG ask and requires courage.

1. What key amends do you need to make? What would you ideally like to see happen as a result? What do you think could realistically happen initially, and also up the road?

The Heart of the Matter

9 Anyone who claims to be in the light but hates his brother is still in the darkness. 10 Whoever loves his brother lives in the light, and there is nothing in him to make him stumble. 11 But whoever hates his brother is in the darkness and walks around in the darkness; he does not know where he is going, because darkness has blinded him. 1 JOHN 2:9-11 NIV

34 For out of the overflow of the heart the mouth speaks. 35 The good man brings good things out of the good stored up in him, and the evil man brings evil things out of the evil stored up in him. 36 But I tell you that men will have to give an account on the day of judgment for every careless word they have spoken. 37 For by your words you will be acquitted, and by your words you will be condemned. MATTHEW 12:34-37 NIV

2. What are two indicators that we're not yet prepared to forgive (1 John 2:9 and Matthew 12:34)? Where must we focus to move ahead?

3. What are the two motivations given in (1 John 2:10-11 and Matthew 12:36-37) for heart change? What are we accountable for?

No Wiggle Room

So, we go back to God to help us walk in His light and love. We deal with our hurts and resentments before God. Who then is responsible to take care of making things right?

21 You're familiar with the command to the ancients, "Do not murder." 22 I'm telling you that anyone who is so much as angry with his brother or sister is guilty of murder. Carelessly call your brother "idiot" and you might just find yourself hauled into court. Thoughtlessly yell "stupid!" at your sister and you are on the brink of hellfire. The simple moral fact is that words kill. 23 This is how I want you to conduct yourselves in these matters. If you enter your place of worship and, about to make an offering, you suddenly remember a grudge a friend has against you, 24 abandon your offering, leave immediately, go to this friend and make things right. Then, and only then, come back and work things out with God. MATTHEW 5:21-24 MESSAGE

25 And whenever you stand praying, if you have anything against anyone, forgive him, so that your Father in heaven will also forgive you your wrongdoing. 26 But if you don't forgive, neither will your Father in heaven forgive your wrongdoing.

MARK 11:25-26 HCSB

4. We've discussed the power of our words before, but how does Jesus view this (Matthew 5:22-23)?

5. What priority does Jesus give to the health of our relationships as compared to our worship and offerings (Matthew 5:23-24 and Mark 11:25)? In what ways should this affect our lives and relationships?

6. Who does Jesus hold responsible for trying to make things right when you have hurt someone and he or she has a grudge against you (Matthew 5:23)? How about when it is you who has been wronged by somebody (Mark 11:25)?

LEADER: *Invite volunteers to read the key elements for making amends and related Bible passages. Watch your time. Group members will have this list to refer back to.*

HOW TO MAKE AMENDS

The specific approach to making amends will vary for each set of people and circumstances, but there are some key elements the Bible lays out for this process.

(1) Accept God's forgiveness: We can love because God first loved, and we can forgive because God has forgiven us so much. Live in His forgiveness, and remember, this is no more condemnation for those living in Christ (Romans 8:1).

(2) Approach the other person with a loving attitude: Pray that the Holy Spirit will fill you with love and give you His eyes to see the other person's perspective. Don't expect instant forgiveness. Sometimes it's easy, and sometimes it's a long journey.

(3) Apologize for the harm you've caused: If there is any way possible, do this face to face. Think through beforehand what you want to say or do. Be specific in naming your specific offenses. Keep it simple and direct. Drop your mask at least a little, and share from your heart about your regrets.

(4) Keep this about your part in the situation: Remember that it's always possible to find fault in other people, but this is about dealing with your issues, not theirs. This is where humility and gentleness come in again. Don't get defensive or start blaming.

(5) Be willing to accept the consequences of your actions: Our apologies, changes, good intentions, and restitutions can't necessarily remove the hurt and damage our past attitudes and behavior have caused. While God has removed the guilt and shame of our failures, there are still consequences that we'll have to find a way to live with.

(6) Make restitution: Restitution is doing what you need to do to make things as right as you can through replacing or restoring what you took away from the other person. Be sure to think through this ahead of time; seek counsel if you're unsure what to do.

(7) Don't do more damage: Make amends, "except when to do so would injure them or others." We must not damage others for our recovery. Typically we avoid in-person amends to remarried ex-spouses, and we always avoid dragging others down in cases of marital infidelity. Exposing infidelity can be extremely destructive, and must always be discussed first with an experienced counselor. In other cases, the offended person's wounds may still be too fresh, with more time required. Lastly, some situations may be just too torturous for us to handle in person or until more healing has occurred.

NOTE: Change the offending behavior: To offer an apology is one thing, to change the offending behavior will demonstrate the integrity of that apology. We *do* need to verbalize our apologies, but the expressions, "talk is cheap" and "actions speak louder than words" are popular because our world is full of empty apologies

DIVINELY POWERFUL WEAPON: RESTITUTION

Making amends is never just about words. Earlier in Matthew 12:24 we discovered that our words come "out of the overflow of the heart"? Making amends is all about the new life that overflows out of our renewed hearts.

If we look at the story of Zacchaeus, we'll find a guy who shows us how to make amends the right way. Zacchaeus was a tax collector in the city of Jericho. Tax collectors were hated by the people because they became wealthy through deceit, abuse, and extortion.

Zacchaeus stood up and said to the Lord, "Look Lord! Here and now I give half of my possessions to the poor, and if I have cheated anybody out of anything, I will pay back four times the amount."

LUKE 19:8 NIV

7. As you read Zacchaeus' words, what do you imagine has occurred in his heart?

8. Jewish law addressed the issue of making restitution, but only required like repayment. But Zacchaeus went above and beyond restitution. How do you think people responded to Zacchaeus' commitment to make amends? What can we learn from this?

EMBRACING THE TRUTH - 25 MINUTES

LEADER: *To help group members integrate and apply the truths about making amends into their own recovery, it's important to deal with fears before approaching a person to make amends. With the fear out of the way, forgiveness is accessible. Take time to stop during "Embracing the Truth," and discuss any points that need clarifying.*

FEAR FACTOR

When we seek to forgive those who have hurt us, and even more so when we go to ask other's forgiveness, there is risk involved.

1. Think about the priority people on your amends list. As you consider approaching these people, do you have any worries or fears? Describe one or two to the group.

The primary fear factor is the inescapable truth that we are not in control of how the other person responds. Contemplating of the sting of rejection or even ridicule are enormous hurdles to completing the amends process! If our first attempts are bad experiences, we may easily decide never to try again. Skipping the amends process is not a good option because it leaves unresolved issues festering in our hearts.

THE GOLDEN RULE

Most of us know the Golden Rule: "Do unto others as you would have others do unto you." Let's look at this in a more contemporary version of Luke 6:31:

[27] To you who are ready to hear the truth, I say this: Love your enemies. Let them bring out the best in you, not the worst. [28] When someone gives you a hard time, respond with the energies of prayer for that person. [29] If someone slaps you in the face, stand there and take it. If someone grabs your shirt, giftwrap your best coat and make a present of it. [30] If someone takes unfair advantage of you, use the occasion to practice the servant life. No more tit for tat stuff. Live generously. [31] Here's a simple rule of thumb for behavior: Ask yourself what you want people to do for you; then grab the initiative and do it for them!

LUKE 6:27-31 MESSAGE

2. Jesus' ways of doing things run counter to just about everything in our culture. What response in Luke 6:27-31 hit you as the most radical?

PREPARING FOR THE WORST

Experience teaches us that to consider the worst case scenario prepares us best. Then, if things go well or at best awkwardly, we're ready, and we've thought through our response. NOTE: If people on your list have died or cannot be located, writing a letter is a big help.

BLOWN OFF: If they ignore me and my attempt at reconciliation, the worst thing that can happen is that I'll feel more _____!

If someone refuses to hear you out, it can feel like the worst kind of rejection. He or she may not be ready to deal with the pain yet. This is only fair. The person may need more time, or some space to process what you're trying to do. This is all good! The person might also be just totally fed up with you because of past hurts and attempts to apologize.

3. As a group, brainstorm effective responses and alternative approaches.

BLOWN UP: If they explode with anger because I'm trying to make amends, the worst thing that can happen is that I'll feel more _____!

It may backfire and the other person may go off on you like a bomb. "Who are you to ask me to forgive you? Who am I, God or something to forgive you at this stage of the game, when you've hurt me so much?" When this happens, it's time to take it — it's a test of your humility and sincerity. If you're defensive and angered, you need to regroup and step back to Step 4 to look at any false beliefs and Step 7 for repentance and restoration.

4. If the main response is an explosion of anger, what does that tell you about the weight of the offense? As a group, brainstorm effective responses and alternative approaches.

BLOWN OUT: If they discredit my effort and point to other times I've seemed sincere, but was either being manipulative or just fell right back into my old ways, the worst thing that can happen is that I'll feel more _____!

Take your time, and plan the best time and place to approach people you think will have this response. Understand that they may not believe you because of past experiences. You will need to prove yourself to them. Time will be your best ally.

5. What lesson can you learn from Zacchaeus that would help you prove your sincerity?

BLOWN AWAY: If they accept my simple and sincere attempt, and become willing to work with me, I would feel _____!

Be grateful for another shot at reconciliation; this is a sign of the grace of God at work. To go to the next level in the relationship, some degree of trust will have been restored. Relational and behavioral boundaries are needed. Ask each person willing to work with you toward reconciliation what boundaries they believe would help.

CONNECTING - 20 MINUTES

> **LEADER:** *The discussions in the "Connecting" time will focus on our attitudes as we step out to make amends, as well as the enabling power of Jesus and the Holy Spirit, who live and move in our lives. Encourage group members to be very supportive of each other as they tackle the sometimes difficult task of making amends.*

PEACEMAKERS

²⁹ Watch the way you talk. Let nothing foul or dirty come out of your mouth. Say only what helps, each word a gift. ³⁰ Don't grieve God. Don't break his heart. His Holy Spirit, moving and breathing in you, is the most intimate part of your life, making you fit for himself. Don't take such a gift for granted. ³¹ Make a clean break with all cutting, backbiting, profane talk. ³² Be gentle with one another, sensitive. Forgive one another as quickly and thoroughly as God in Christ forgave you.

EPHESIANS 4:29-32 MESSAGE

1. Who joins us when we go to make amends (Ephesians 4:30)? Where exactly are they?

2. What attitudes and behaviors are identified in these passages that can block the power of Jesus and the Spirit in our relationships? How can we get in the way of our own healing?

3. As we allow the Spirit to work in and through us, what are some specific attitudes and actions highlighted as relationship-builders in Ephesians 4:29-32 and Galatians 2:20?

4. Which Spirit-grieving attitudes or actions from question 2 do you tend to struggle with most? What do you think needs to change in you so you're less apt to break God's heart in your dealings with people?

If it is possible, as far as it depends on you, live at peace with everyone. ROMANS 12:18 NIV

Finally, brothers, rejoice. Be restored, be encouraged, be of the same mind, be at peace, and the God of love and peace will be with you.

2 CORINTHIANS 13:11 HCSB

Blessed are the peacemakers, because they will be called sons of God. MATTHEW 5:9 HCSB

5. How important do you think making peace is in God's view of life? What level of priority and effort does He expect from us? What promises does God make to peacemakers in 2 Corinthians 13:11 and Matthew 5:9?

6. What could we miss out on if we're not committed to the process of making amends, of reconciling relationships?

How can we support you practically and in prayer as you press on in making amends?

MY PRAYER REQUESTS & NEEDS:

MY GROUP'S PRAYER REQUESTS & NEEDS:

CLOSING RECOVERY PRAYER:
Holy Spirit, would you, throughout this week, fill us to overflowing with Your love and grace, so that Your life will flow out of us to those we need to meet? Give us the grace and strength to deal patiently and gently with these people we've harmed or cheated.

TAKING IT HOME

LEADER: *The primary focus of "Taking it Home" this week is to dive into Step 9 and take initial steps to make amends with the top people on our lists. Encourage optimism and realistic.*

A QUESTION TO TAKE TO MY HEART:

Search deep into your heart to answer the following question. This is a time for introspection and reflection; it's a time to grapple with what beliefs in your innermost being really drive your thinking and behavior.

✱ What hesitation do I have in seeking forgiveness and making amends with the top people on my list? What are my greatest fears? What's really driving those fears or anxieties?

MY STORY: Trust in the Holy Spirit to open your eyes & heart as you write.

1. What do I think is the best way and time to approach my top three people?

2. How do I think each of my top three is likely to respond to my effort to make amends?

3. How did each of my top three actually respond to my initial effort to make amends? How am I feeling about that?

Although making amends could be a long-term process, I've begun the process of making amends with all of the top priority people on my list.

Signed _____   Date: _____

RELAPSE
PREVENTION (STEP 10)

BREAKING THE ICE - 15 MINUTES

LEADER: *This "Breaking the Ice" time will begin on a more serious note to allow you to discuss how the initial steps in making amends went for each group member. After that you'll use a lighter group experience as a lead-in to discussions about Step 10 in our 12-Step recovery process. Be sure everyone gets a turn, but keep things moving. Impromptu prayer is appropriate for deep hurts.*

Let's start off by discussing how your amends process is going.

1. Share your best highlight so far as you've started to make amends. What has been your strongest encouragement? Biggest disappointment? Greatest struggles?

LEADER INSTRUCTIONS FOR GROUP EXPERIENCE: *Read the paragraph that follows, and show the clip from the Disney-animated movie* The Hunchback of Notre Dame. *In this scene Quasimodo is bound, but freed by Esmeralda, who also needs help to get to freedom. Show the first half of scene 9 that runs from 27:27 to 30:08 minutes on the DVD. Stop the video just after Esmeralda disappears for good the second time.*

Quasimodo is the lonely bell ringer of Notre Dame. He finds security in his tower, but eventually risks venturing out of the tower into freedom and into his first friendship with a gypsy named Esmeralda. At first he enjoys his freedom, but then he ends up bound and mistreated. In his pain and bondage, he calls out to his friend for help.

2. After Quasimodo called for help and Esmeralda came to his aid, what were the various sources of help and unconventional weapons that secured the freedom of Quasimodo and Esmeralda?

3. Quasimodo was unaware of the danger around him when he first found freedom from the tower, but he was clearly aware of the danger in this scene. Did you notice the old man that was released from the cage? What happened to him? What things did Quasimodo have going for him that this man was lacking?

4. What parallels do you see between this scene and elements of our Recovery Map?

Opening Prayer:

Father, You have brought us this far. Help us focus on new habits that will keep us on the path of light and freedom. We want to continue to live in Your light and freedom.

In Step 9: We actively began to make amends with people we have offended or hurt.

In Step 10: We've come a long way on our journey to recovery, healing, and freedom. But our initial breaking free is the beginning of our story, not the end. We will discuss strategies for relapse prevention.

Objectives for this Step:

- Realize the real danger of falling back into our well-worn paths of addiction
- Grasp the importance of making Steps 4-9 an ongoing way of life – we continue living out of our new heart
- Learn practical relapse prevention strategies

Discovering the Truth - 40 minutes

With Step 10, we enter the "Sticking with It" stage in our Recovery Map: BE PREVENTATIVE: We continue to take personal inventory, and proactively live out of our new heart. When we are wrong, we promptly admit it, and turn back to truth and light.

Recovery Map

STARTING WITH DECISION	1. Admit your need
	2. Find new power
	3. Make a decision
SEARCHING MY SELF	4. Take inventory
	5. Admit your addiction to others
	6. Prepare for change
SEEKING HEALING & CHANGE	7. Ask God to restore & redeem life
	8. Identify resentments & offenses
	9. Make amends
STICKING WITH IT	10. Be preventative
	11. Stay connected with God
	12. Share your story

The Relapse Trap

Freeing ourselves from addictions and false beliefs has been a theme throughout "Stopping the Madness." By now, you should be walking in some measure of freedom. That's why we're here: to see our lives transformed and keep moving toward freedom from addiction, our distorted passions, and those well-worn paths and destructive habit patterns. A quick fix is comparable to a fad diet that we can't maintain. We've been in the process of working with God to overhaul our hearts and lives. To be successful as we continue our journey, we'll need to continue to live out of our new hearts, and form new, constructive habit patterns.

Let him who thinks he stands take heed that he does not fall.

1 CORINTHIANS 10:12 NASB

[8] Be of sober spirit, be on the alert. Your adversary, the devil, prowls around like a roaring lion, seeking someone to devour. [9] But resist him, firm in your faith, knowing that the same experiences of suffering are being accomplished by your brethren who are in the world.

1 PETER 5:8-9 NASB

1. What's the key message of 1 Corinthians 10:12 and 1 Peter 5:8? Will we ever be free from temptation and the need to fight to retain the freedom we attain?

PREVENT Strategy 1: Prepare

Seven strategies built around the word "PREVENT" will be our allies as we resist the enemy and temptations from our own distorted desires. The first strategy is advance preparation. We cannot wait for a fire to be blazing before we figure out how we're going to put it out!

Prepare your minds for action; be self-controlled; set your heart fully on the grace to be given you when Jesus is revealed.

1 PETER 1:3 NIV

[15] Pay careful attention, then, how you walk—not as unwise people, but as wise— [16] making the most of the time, because the days are evil. [17] So don't be foolish, but understand what the Lord's will is.

EPHESIANS 5:15-17 HCSB

2. What are some ways highlighted in 1 Peter 1:3 and Ephesians 5:15-17 that will help us prepare before we face the temptations that will come?

PREVENT Strategy 2: Review and recycle

Steps 4-9 in our Recovery Map need to become a way of life for us. The 12 Steps of our Recovery Map need to be our constant companion. We must continue to take personal inventory, and proactively live out of our new heart. When we are wrong, we promptly admit it, and turn back to truth and light. Taking our personal inventory should be (1) ongoing each time any issue crops up, (2) daily in our time alone with God, and (3) part of a formal tune-up every 6 to 12 months.

Watch out that you do not lose what you have worked for, but that you may be rewarded fully.

2 John 8 niv

3. Some believe that a relapse every now and then is good for you. How does God view relapse prevention in 2 John 8? What are some ways we can make taking a personal inventory a habit?

PREVENT Strategy 3: Envision Our Future Glory

It's easy to get bogged down in the routine and struggles, to keep our focus on our needs and desires. Our culture expects instant gratification, quick fixes, and ease. We must refocus on the larger story, living and longing for all that awaits us.

[16] We are children of God, [17] and if children, heirs also, heirs of God and fellow heirs with Christ, if indeed we suffer with Him so that we may be glorified with Him. [18] For I consider that the sufferings of this present time are not worthy to be compared with the glory that is to be revealed to us. [19] For the anxious longing of all creation waits eagerly for the revealing of the sons of God.

Romans 8:16-19 nasb

4. What value is keeping the eternal vision and plan of God constantly before our eyes? What are some practical things we can do individually and as groups of "heirs of God" to keep our focus on the larger story?

PREVENT Strategy 4: Value My Heart

We have focused on the importance of our hearts throughout our recovery. Remember, each of our behaviors are rooted in a belief we hold in our hearts. If we value and guard our hearts, we will set boundaries to protect them, and keep our heart connected to God.

Above all else guard your heart, for it is the wellspring of life.

Proverbs 4:23 niv

⁹ How can a young man keep his way pure? By keeping Your word. ¹⁰ I have sought You with all my heart; don't let me wander from Your [God's] commands. ¹¹ I have treasured Your word in my heart so that I may not sin against You. ... ¹⁵ I will meditate on Your precepts and think about Your ways. ¹⁶ I will delight in Your statutes; I will not forget Your word.

PSALM 119:9-11,15-16 NASB

5. Why is it so important to guard our hearts rather than just being focused on controlling our behavior (Proverbs 4:23)? What are some ways that we stay connected with our hearts and with God (Psalm 119)?

PREVENT STRATEGY 5: ESCAPE TEMPTATION

There are times that temptation jumps right into our laps and there's no way we can avoid it. In our world, temptations are everywhere. When you find yourself in a tempting situation, lace up your Nikes®, turn, and run in the opposite direction as fast as you can!

¹² Let him who thinks he stands take heed that he does not fall. ¹³ No temptation has overtaken you but such is common to man; and God will not allow you to be tempted beyond what you are able, but with the temptation will provide the way of escape also, so that you will be able to endure it.

1 CORINTHIANS 10:12-13 NASB

6. What false beliefs can prevent us from taking the escape hatch that God always provides with temptation (1 Corinthians 10:13)? What are some ways that we can continue to transform these false beliefs?

PREVENT STRATEGY 6: NO PROVISION FOR THE FLESH

If we spit into the wind, we're going to regret it. If we eat contaminated food, no matter how good it tastes, we're going to pay for it dearly. If we waltz into a lion's den, it's unlikely we'll come out alive. It makes no sense to put ourselves in a position where we will fall back into our old ways and addictions.

¹² The night is almost gone, and the day is near. Therefore let us lay aside the deeds of the darkness and put on the armor of light. ¹³ Let us behave properly as in the day, not in carousing and drunkenness, not in sexual promiscuity and sensuality, not in strife and jealousy. ¹⁴ But put on the Lord Jesus Christ, and make no provision for the flesh in regard to its lusts.

ROMANS 13:12-14 NASB

[6] *Let no one deceive you with empty words, for because of such things God's wrath comes on those who are disobedient.* *[7]* *Therefore do not be partners with them.* *[8]* *For you were once in darkness, but now you are light in the Lord. Live as children of light ... [10] and find out what pleases the Lord.* *[11]* *Have nothing to do with the fruitless deeds of darkness, but rather expose them.*

EPHESIANS 5:6-8,10-11 NIV

7. The "flesh" is that alien force we still carry inside—the distorted desires and old habit patterns. What does "make no provision for the flesh" (Romans 13:14) mean? What does this require of us?

8. Give some examples of practical steps we can take to "lay aside the deeds or darkness" (Romans 13:12) and "live as children of light" (Ephesians 5:8)?

PREVENT STRATEGY 7: TEAMWORK AND ACCOUNTABILITY

Throughout the life of this group, we've learned the value of a community of people who can hold and help each other up. The temptation, when we complete our pass through the 12 Steps, is to try to go it alone again. The enemy would like nothing more than to isolate us again so he can drag us back into the sewer.

[24] *Let us consider how we spur one another on toward love and good deeds.* *[25]* *Let us not give up meeting together, as some are in the habit of doing, but let us encourage one another—all the more as you see the Day approaching.*

HEBREWS 10:24-25 NASB

[19] *My dear friends, if you know people who have wandered off from God's truth, don't write them off. Go after them.* *[20]* *Get them back and you will have rescued precious lives from destruction and prevented an epidemic of wandering away from God.*

JAMES 5:19-20 MESSAGE

9. What are ways we can we be there for each other after completing our 12 Steps? With whom can you or have you developed a no pretenses accountability relationship?

$\underline{P}$REPARE

$\underline{R}$EVIEW AND RECYCLE

$\underline{E}$NVISION OUR FUTURE GLORY

$\underline{V}$ALUE MY HEART

$\underline{E}$SCAPE TEMPTATION

$\underline{N}$O PROVISION FOR THE FLESH

$\underline{T}$EAMWORK AND ACCOUNTABILITY

EMBRACING THE TRUTH - 20 MINUTES

> **LEADER:** *Lots of practical application discussion already occurred in "Discovering the Truth." "Embracing the Truth" will help group members understand that the 7 PREVENT strategies will only be successful if our hearts are fully God's. Removing an addiction leaves a gaping hole that must be filled with the right stuff.*

SWEPT CLEAN

Addictions and recovery issues seem to travel in packs of three. Think about the teen who cuts herself as a release for her inner pain. This becomes highly addictive as she feels a release and high from the cutting. Then she admits that she also has an eating disorder. Her desire to control eating seems to be the only thing she can control in her life. As time goes on and she feels trust with the group she explains that the root of it all was the sexual abuse she suffered for five years from her stepfather. Addictions are not simple, and freedom from addictions is never just a matter of sweeping your life clean of the addiction.

[21] When a strong man, fully armed, guards estate, his possessions are secure. [22] But when one stronger than he attacks and overpowers him, he takes all his weapons he trusted in, and divides up his plunder. ... [24] When an unclean spirit comes out of a man, it roams through waterless places looking for rest, then it says, "I'll go back to the house I came from." [25] And returning, it finds [the house] swept and put in order. [26] Then it goes and brings seven other spirits more evil than itself, and they enter and settle down there. As a result, that man's last condition is worse than the first.

LUKE 11:21-22,24-26 HCSB

1. In Luke 21, Jesus uses the image of a house to reflect our hearts and lives. How does the principle of the "one stronger" apply to our lives and addictions? How effective are the weapons we trust in when the enemy in our story attacks (verses 21-22)?

2. In verses 24-26, when an unclean spirit leaves a person, what does it find when it returns? Why do you think sweeping the house clean and putting it back in order didn't keep the unclean spirit from returning?

3. Read Luke 11:21-26 again. When we look at sweeping our "unclean spirit" or addiction out of our lives, how can we prevent the evil thing from returning with worse evils to terrorize and bind us? How can we resist the "strong man"?

The seven PREVENT strategies will serve you well, but not if try to use your own personal weapons – you need the divinely powerful weapons you've had experience with now (2 Corinthians 10:4-5). But the Strongest One's weapons aren't even enough – you need Him to wield those weapons on your behalf.

There's a principle in the physical realm that Jesus also applied to the spiritual realm: nature abhors a vacuum. Removing any addiction or old habit pattern leaves a gaping hole that must be filled with the something strong and constructive. Ephesians 4:22-24 and 5:17-18 give more insight into filling the vacuum.

17 Don't be foolish, but understand what the Lord's will is. 18 And don't get drunk with wine, which [leads to] reckless actions, but be filled with the Spirit.

EPHESIANS 5:17-18 HCSB

22 You were taught, with regard to your former way of life, to put off your old self, which is being corrupted by its deceitful desires; 23 to be made new in the attitude of your minds; 24 and to put on the new self, created to be like God in true righteousness and holiness.

EPHESIANS 4:22-24 NIV

4. Why is being filled with the Spirit compared to being drunk? What is affected by drunkenness? According to verse 17, what's required of us to experience this filling?

5. Both teachings in Ephesians talk about truth of replacement that Jesus alluded to in Luke 11. What do we need to put off? What do we need to put on? How often do we need to make these replacements?

CONNECTING - 20 MINUTES

LEADER INSTRUCTIONS FOR GROUP EXPERIENCE: *Show the second clip from the Disney-animated movie* The Hunchback of Notre Dame. *Play scene 24 (1:12:56 minutes on the DVD) and continue part way into scene 25. This clip begins where Esmeralda is now caught and bound, and this time Quasimodo comes to her aid. The battle rages as Phoebus leads the people against the evil Frollo. Stop after the old man from the first clip gets free but then falls into the sewer (at 1:16:13 minutes on the DVD).*

THE LARGER STORY

In this scene, it's Esmeralda who needs someone to help free her, and this time we see the larger battle of good vs. evil played out in a dramatic way. Much more is at stake for all those people trapped in captivity to evil and all those that could become imprisoned or destroyed.

1. Quasimodo is trapped again and despairing. What shakes him up enough to break free? What motivates the people under the leadership of Phoebus to join in the battle?

2. How did focusing on the larger story and rallying together affect both the larger battle and each individual battle? What did the captives who were set free do?

3. The old man finally got freed again from the stocks. Where did he end up this time? What lessons should he have learned from his previous relapse into captivity, but obviously didn't?

MY STORY

4. How hard has it been to give up your addiction or "drug of choice"? How concerned are you about relapse?

5. What are your personal warning signs? How can you tell if an urge or a binge is on its way? How can others around you tell something's up?

6. What has become your number one relapse prevention technique so far? What can you say without a doubt is working for you?

How can we help support you practically and specifically this week as you continue to fight for your freedom? How can this group pray for you?

MY PRAYER REQUESTS & NEEDS:

MY GROUP'S PRAYER REQUESTS & NEEDS:

CLOSING RECOVERY PRAYER:

Holy Spirit, fill us full of You this week. As we continue to clean our "house" and put it in order, help us to replace the junk with the good gifts You supply. Remind us to put off the old self and put on the new self, using the PREVENT strategies and Your powerful weapons to keep the house clean.

TAKING IT HOME

MY STORY: Trust in the Holy Spirit to open your eyes & heart as you write.

[1] Since Jesus went through everything you're going through and more, learn to think like him. Think of your suffering as a weaning from the old sinful habit of always expecting to get your own way. [2] Then you'll be able to live out your days free to pursue what God wants instead of being tyrannized by what you want. [3] You've already put in your time in that God-ignorant way of life, partying night after night, a drunken and profligate life. Now it's time to be done with it for good. [4] Of course, your old friends don't understand why you don't join in with the old gang anymore. [5] But you don't have to give and account to them. They're the ones who will be called on the carpet—and before God himself.

1 PETER 4:1-5 MESSAGE

We've seen the danger of leaving a vacuum in our lives, and we've studied the principle of replacement. What are some old destructive habits you need to dump? Spend time in prayer and ask God what new habits you'll need as replacements. Make a list like this in your journal:

Destructive Habit:

_____

_____

_____

_____

_____

_____

_____

_____

_____

Replacement Habit:

_____

_____

_____

_____

_____

_____

_____

_____

_____

A QUESTION TO TAKE TO GOD:

✳ God, how does it make You feel when I relapse and turn back to my addiction or fall back into my old ruts? How do You really feel about me in those times when I blow it?

IDEAS FOR YOUR DAILY JOURNAL:

- Triggers for my relapses and near-relapses
- PREVENT strategies that are most effective for me
- Transformations God is making in my heart and mind
- Victories AND temporary setbacks

KEEPING GOD IN MY STORY (STEP II)

BREAKING THE ICE - 10 MINUTES

> **LEADER:** *The "Breaking the Ice" questions for this session will continue to deepen relationships in the group, and allow group members dream a little, and share a bit about their earthly fathers. Be sure everyone gets a turn, but keep things moving. Let this time be light, fun, and encouraging.*

1. If you were handed Aladdin's magic lamp, what three wishes would you make? Be outrageous with your third wish; dream big.

2. When you were a child, what was the most exciting outing you had with your father or someone who was a father figure to you? Why was it so memorable?

3. When you were a child, what was the most frightening thing to you? Who did you run to that made you feel safe when you experienced that fear?

4. How did your "Taking it Home" assignment go? What did you hear from God about your relapses—how He feels about them, and about you?

Opening Prayer:

Holy Spirit, show us that freedom is attainable and that we can live a life of joy in You. We cannot do this alone and are aware that it will require a constant conscious walk with You. We ask that You reveal something new of Yourself to each of us today.

In Step 10: We focused on how to stick with our recovery, and build toward more and more healing and freedom. We discussed The PREVENT strategies for relapse prevention, and keyed in on the need to be filled with the Spirit, replacing hurtful, destruction habits with godly, constructive habits.

In Step 11: We continue to set our sights on sticking with our recovery process. Grasping and going deeper in our relationship with God is the key to staying free, and finding true fulfillment in our lives.

Objectives for this Step:

- Embrace the truth that we need God directing our story to keep us free
- Be overwhelmed by the depth of God's love for each of us
- Embrace our favored position as children of God and heirs destined for glory
- Understand and commit to our part in pursuing God
- Recognize how God delights in us, and how He pursues us
- Learn to rest in the unforced rhythms of God's grace

DISCOVERING THE TRUTH - 20 MINUTES

LEADER *Invite group members to read various explanations and Bible passages. "Discovering the Truth" helps group members understand the importance of God in our stories, and discuss the depth of God's love and the privileged position God has freely given us. Watch your time here!*

Step 11 is another vital element to help us stick with the gains we've made, and press on even farther in our Recovery Map: STAY CONNECTED WITH GOD: We seek through listening prayer, Bible study, and heart transformation, to keep improving our relationship with God, seeking His presence, direction, and power in our lives.

RECOVERY MAP

STARTING WITH	1	1. Admit your need
DECISION	2	2. Find new power
	3	3. Make a decision
SEARCHING	4	4. Take inventory
MY SELF	5	5. Admit your addiction to others
	6	6. Prepare for change
SEEKING HEALING	7	7. Ask God to restore & redeem life
& CHANGE	8	8. Identify resentments & offenses
	9	9. Make amends
STICKING	10	10. Be preventative
WITH IT	11	**11. Stay connected with God**
	12	12. Share your story

WE NEED THE HERO IN OUR STORY

We recognized in Steps 1 and 2 that we were powerless over our addictions and needed God's power to make life manageable again. We were captives in need of a rescuer. We still need the Hero in our story to preserve our hard-fought freedom.

[7] But we have this treasure in clay jars to show that this all-surpassing power is from God and not from us. [8] We are hard pressed one every side, but not crushed; perplexed but not in despair; [9] persecuted but not abandoned, struck down but not destroyed.

2 CORINTHIANS 4:7-9 NIV

[31] Jesus said ... "If you continue in My word, you really are My disciples. [32] You will know the truth, and the truth will set you free."

JOHN 8:31-32 HCSB

1. In what ways can you relate to Paul's struggles in 2 Corinthians 4:8-9? What keeps life from caving in on us (verse 7)?

2. What would complete freedom look like to you? According to John 8:31-32, what makes us free, and how do we obtain it?

GOD'S HEART TOWARD YOU

If we're going to trust God to direct our story, then we need to truly understand His heart toward us. There are often doubts in our hearts about whether God really cares.

The LORD your God is with you, he is mighty to save. He will take great delight in you, he will quiet you with His love, he will rejoice over you with singing.

ZEPHANIAH 3:17 NIV

[God speaking:] ¹⁵ "Can a woman forget her nursing child, or lack compassion for the child of her womb? Even if these forget, yet I will not forget you. ¹⁶ Look, I have inscribed you on the palms of My hands.

ISAIAH 49:15-16 HCSB

3. Sure God loves everybody because He's God. But how personal is His love for each of His children—for you — according to Zephaniah 3:17 and Isaiah 49:15-16?

4. How does it make you feel that God has inscribed your name in the palm of His hand where you are always before His eyes? What are the things that make you hesitant to fully accept that God really delights in you (Zephaniah 3:17)?

YOUR FAVORED POSITION IN GOD'S FAMILY

God's love has been lavished upon those who place their faith in Jesus. Because of nothing other than God's extreme love for us, we have been given a position that few of us have grasped, and even fewer live in. Our enemy clearly wants to keep this hidden.

¹⁴ All those led by God's Spirit are God's sons. ¹⁵ For you did not receive a spirit of slavery to fall back into fear, but you received the Spirit of adoption, by whom we cry out, "Abba, Father!" ¹⁶ The Spirit Himself testifies together with our spirit that we are God's children, ¹⁷ and if children, also heirs—heirs of God and co-heirs with Christ —seeing that we suffer with Him so that we may also be glorified with Him.

ROMANS 8:14-17 HCSB

¹ If you have been raised up with Christ, keep seeking the things above, where Christ is, seated at the right hand of God. ² Set your mind on the things above, not on the things that are on earth. ³ For you have died and your life is hidden with Christ in God. ⁴ When Christ, who is our life, is revealed, then you also will be revealed with Him in glory.

COLOSSIANS 3:1-4 NASB

5. What amazing privileges do each of us receive when we become children of God, with the full status of a first-born son (Romans 8:14-17 and Colossians 3:1-4)?

We've already been granted the privileges of sonship, but our position as royalty will not be fully revealed until Jesus returns in His glory. As His followers, we participate spiritually in His death, His resurrection, and His glorification.

6. How might embracing our favored status affect the way we approach life, the enemy, and our enslavement to addictions (Romans 8:15,17 and Colossians 3:2)?

EMBRACING THE TRUTH - 35 MINUTES

> **LEADER:** *"Discovering the Truth" was a little shorter because "Embracing the Truth" will need extra time to discuss our pursuit of God, and also how God pursues us.*

OUR PURSUIT OF GOD

To deepen our relationship with God, we need to be pursuing Him.

¹ As the deer pants for streams of water, so my soul pants for you, O God. ² My soul thirsts for the living God. When can I go and meet with God?

PSALM 42:1-2 NIV

¹³ Don't look for shortcuts to God. The market is flooded with sure-fire, easygoing formulas for a successful life that can be practiced in your spare time. Don't fall for that stuff, even though crowds of people do. ¹⁴ The way to life—to God!—is vigorous and requires total attention.

MATTHEW 7:13-14 MESSAGE

⁷ Keep asking, and it will be given to you. Keep searching, and you will find. Keep knocking, and the door will be opened to you. ⁸ For everyone who asks receives, and the one who searches finds, and to the one who knocks, the door will be opened.

MATTHEW 7:7-8 HCSB

¹⁶ Therefore we do not lose heart. Though outwardly we are wasting away, yet inwardly we are being renewed day by day. ¹⁷ For our light and momentary troubles are achieving for us an eternal glory that far outweighs them all. ¹⁸ So we fix our eyes not on what is seen, but on what is unseen. For what is seen is temporary, but what is unseen is eternal.

2 CORINTHIANS 4:16-18

1. Each of these four passages has emotion and passion; that's what God desires from us. What key passion do you see in each of the following verses? How is it demonstrated?

   Psalm 42:1-2: _____

   _____

   Matthew 7:13-14: _____

   _____

   Matthew 7:7-8: _____

   _____

   2 Corinthians 4:16-18: _____

   _____

2. What is God's promise in Matthew 7:7-8 as we continue to pursue Him as an ongoing way of life?

3. What is the motivation for us to press on in our journey through the hard things of life (2 Corinthians 4:16-18)? What do we have to look forward to? How do the struggles we experience in this life compare to the unseen reality?

GOD'S PURSUIT OF US

We discovered how much God really enjoys each one of us. He also longs for a deep relationship with us all. That's a new revelation to many of us.

The Song of Songs is a love poem that beautifully illustrates marital love as God intended it, but it also powerfully depicts the love of God for His people. God often uses the marriage and parenting illustrations to help us understand the depth of His love for us.

8 Listen! My love [is approaching]. Look! Here he comes, leaping over the mountains, bounding over the hills. 9 My love is like a gazelle or a young stag. Look, he is standing behind our wall, gazing through the windows, peering through the lattice. 10 My love calls to me: Arise, my darling. Come away, my beautiful one.

SONG OF SONGS 2:8-10 HCSB

6. The "love" in Song of Songs 2:8-10 allegorically refers to God, and the object of his affection is you. Which words in this poem illustrate God's love toward you? How does this align with your current views of God?

God also uses the illustration of a shepherd to communicate His love and care for us.

He tends His flock like a shepherd: He gathers the lambs in His arms and carries them close to his heart; he gently leads those that have young.

ISAIAH 40:11 NIV

12 As a shepherd looks after his scattered flock when he is with them, so will I look after my sheep. I will rescue them from all the places where they were scattered on a day of clouds and darkness. 15 I myself will tend my sheep and have them lie down, declares the Sovereign LORD. 16 I will search for the lost and bring back the strays. I will bind up the injured and strengthen the weak.

EZEKIEL 34:12,15-16 NIV

7. What is God's approach to leading and caring for you as one of His sheep (Isaiah 40:11)? How does this align with your views about how God treats you?

8. According to Ezekiel 34:12,15-16, how does God deal with us when we get lost in the fog or darkness of life? How does God's promise apply to our own life issues, wounds, addictions, and spiritual struggles?

God is thrilled about you, and longs to see you enthused about life with Him. He also wants us to rest in His arms, comforted in those times when we're unable to pursue God because we're lost, trapped, or struggling. Even then, He's still pursuing us!

CONNECTING - 25 MINUTES

> **LEADER:** *Use this "Connecting" time to help group members begin to understand and accept the depth of God's love, and learn to rest in the comfort of God's grace. Following a discussion about failures, you'll lead a guided prayer experience based on Lamentations 3:22-25 (NIV), Isaiah 55:7 (NASB), and Matthew 11:28-30 (The Message).*

GOD'S RESPONSE TO OUR FAILURES

Failure, relapse, sin, weakness, bondage, hurt, shame, guilt, judgment – all words that make our stomachs churn. God wants us free; we want to be free; others are cheering us on; and still others stand by pointing fingers. We want freedom, but we've blown it, again.

¹⁹ I remember my affliction and my wandering, the bitterness and the gall. ²⁰ I well remember them, and my soul is downcast within me.

LAMENTATIONS 3:19-20 NIV

⁴ For my sins have flooded over my head; they are a burden too heavy for me to bear. ⁵ My wounds are foul and festering because of my foolishness. ⁶ I am bent over and brought low; all day long I go around in mourning. ⁷ For my loins are full of burning pain, and there is no health in my body. ⁸ I am faint and severely crushed; I groan because of the anguish of my heart.

PSALM 38:4-8 HCSB

1. Which feelings and attitudes can you relate to from Lamentations 3:20 and Psalm 38:4-8? How do you respond physically and emotionally when you fail or relapse?

2. How do you think God feels when you fail again? What are the effects of your sin on your relationship with God? How long do these effects typically last for you?

Failure and sin in our lives distresses us all. It robs us of all the good gifts our Father has lavished on us. The enemy of our souls kicks us while we're down. We can easily lose heart and lose hope. All the destructive self-talk kicks in, and before we know it we've fallen back into slavery. God has made a way to demolish this cycle. Let's take some time to address this issue of failures through a "Listening Prayer" exercise.

LISTENING PRAYER TIME:

You're going to lead group members in a short time of listening prayer.
- *Allow this experience some time; don't rush it.*
- *Put on quiet background music (use the CD* Pursued by God: Redemptive Worship Volume 1 *from Serendipity House, or select your own music); dim the lights if possible.*
- *Help each person create a small personal area. This is not a time to chat; make it very honoring.*
- *Trust God to speak to each person individually.*

DIRECTIONS ...

1. Say, *"Our failures and sins tear us up inside, and God could in all fairness consume us with His wrath, but that's not how He treats His children. In Lamentations 3 and Isaiah 55 we find these truths about God ..."* (Read to the group Lamentations 3:22-25 and Isaiah 55:7 on the next page.)

2. Say, *"Ask God to tell you how He feels about you when you relapse."*

3. Say, *"Jesus never expects us to go it alone. In Matthew 11, Jesus says to us ..."* (Read to the group Matthew 11:28-30 on the next page.)

4. Say, *"Did you hear Jesus' offer to you?"* (Reread Matthew 11:28-30.)

5. Say, *"Will you embrace rest, and accept Jesus' offer to walk with Him, work with Him, and learn the unforced rhythms of grace."*

OPTIONAL IDEA ...

Serendipity House produces a resource called FLOOD Volume 2: Distortions. *Either* FLOOD Volume 2 Kit *or* FLOOD Volume 2 DVD-A *contain a powerful short film called "Unforced Rhythms," that's based on Matthew 11:28-30.*

[22] *Because of the L*ORD'*s great love we are not consumed, for his compassions never fail.* [23] *They are new every morning; great is your faithfulness.* [24] *I say to myself, "the L*ORD *is my portion; therefore I will wait for him."* [25] *The Lord is good to those whose hope is in him, to the one who seeks him.*

LAMENTATIONS 3:22-25 NIV

*Let the wicked forsake his way, and the unrighteous man his thoughts; and let him return to the L*ORD*, and He will have compassion on him, and to our God, for He will abundantly pardon.*

ISAIAH 55:7 NASB

[28] *"Are you tired? Worn out? Burned out on religion? Come to me. Get away with me and you'll recover your life. I'll show you how to take a real rest.* [29] *Walk with me and work with me—watch how I do it. Learn the unforced rhythms of grace. I won't lay anything heavy or ill-fitting on you.* [30] *Keep company with me and you'll learn to live freely and lightly."*

MATTHEW 11:28-30 MESSAGE

3. Was there anything God said to you during the "listening prayer"? Share this to encourage the rest of the group.

CLOSING RECOVERY PRAYER:

Jesus, we have struggled so hard with life. We I have fought and strived, we have kicked and screamed. The only time we've stopped fighting is when we've just given up. Keep pursuing us. Keep inviting us to rest in You, walk with You, work You. Our hearts cry out for to live freely and lightly in Your grace.

TAKING IT HOME

THE UNFORCED RHYTHMS OF GRACE

Each day this week, find a peaceful place to be alone with Jesus. Focus on resting with Jesus and walking with Him. Don't push any agenda; just spend together, relax, and wait. Let Jesus drive your recovery at His pace, in His way.

SETTING CAPTIVES FREE (STEP 12)

BREAKING THE ICE - 15 MINUTES

> **LEADER INSTRUCTIONS FOR GROUP EXPERIENCE:** *Show the clip from the DreamWorks-animated movie* **Shrek** *(original movie) in which Shrek tries to explain to the donkey that ogres are like onions. This movie is fun and will get some good discussion going. This clip is in scene 6 and runs from 26:17 to 28:21 minutes on the DVD. Discuss the following questions about the clip.*

1. What do you think Shrek meant by "there's a lot more to ogres than people think"? How do you think people are like onions too?

2. Why do you think Shrek insisted he was like an onion instead of a cake or a parfait? How did you feel about his stubbornness on this point?

3. Do you often feel pressured like Shrek to be something nice and presentable that everybody likes, instead of being true to who you really are? When this happens how do you typically respond?

4. How much time were you able to carve out to spend with Jesus just resting in Him? What was that like for you? Have those times changed you in any way?

OPENING PRAYER:

Jesus, we're learning to rest in You, in the unforced rhythm of grace. We still struggle to understand the depth of Your feelings for us, but we're thankful. Help us as embrace the step of sharing our stories that will complete the cycle of our healing process.

IN STEP 11: We focused on how to stick with our recovery though deepening our relationship with God as the key to staying free, and finding deep fulfillment in our lives.

IN STEP 12: We will discuss the final step in our Recovery Map, which will complete the cycle of our healing process. Our healing deepens as we step outside ourselves, and involve ourselves in the larger story.

OBJECTIVES FOR THIS STEP:

- Accept and appreciate who we really are
- Marvel at what God has for us now and in eternity
- Embrace the vital importance of sharing our story, both for others and for ourselves
- Realize that God loves to use broken and recovering people in His mission of redemption

DISCOVERING THE TRUTH - 35 MINUTES

LEADER: *Invite group members to read various explanations and Bible passages. "Discovering the Truth" helps group members to accept and appreciate who they are, and to begin to realize more about who we were created to be and what unimaginable plans God has for us.*

Step 12 is the final step in our Recovery Map, but's it not the end, but rather a new beginning for us. We need to brand these 12 steps onto our hearts and minds as we continue our journeys. We complete the cycle of healing as we: SHARE OUR STORY OF REDEMPTION: Having experienced a spiritual awakening as a result of these steps, we begin to carry this message of hope and healing to others, as we continue to apply the steps in every area of our lives.

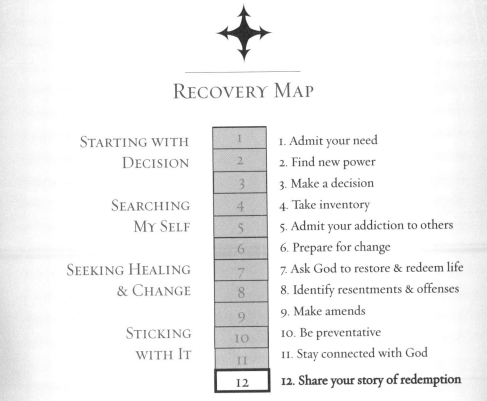

RECOVERY MAP

STARTING WITH	1	1. Admit your need
DECISION	2	2. Find new power
	3	3. Make a decision
SEARCHING	4	4. Take inventory
MY SELF	5	5. Admit your addiction to others
	6	6. Prepare for change
SEEKING HEALING	7	7. Ask God to restore & redeem life
& CHANGE	8	8. Identify resentments & offenses
	9	9. Make amends
STICKING	10	10. Be preventative
WITH IT	11	11. Stay connected with God
	12	**12. Share your story of redemption**

UNLIKELY HEROES

In the video clip of Shrek and Donkey, they were on their way to rescue the princess trapped in a tower, which was guarded by a fire-breathing dragon. These two were certainly unlikely heroes; not exactly Prince Charming or a noble knight in shining armor. But there's a lot more there than meets the eye.

[26] Brothers, consider your calling: not many are wise from a human perspective, not many powerful, not many of noble birth. [27] Instead, God has chosen the world's foolish things to shame the wise, and God has chosen the world's weak things to shame the strong. [28] God has chosen the world's insignificant and despised things—the things viewed as nothing—so He might bring to nothing the things that are viewed as something, [29] so that no one can boast in His presence. [30] But from Him you are in Christ Jesus, who for us became wisdom from God, as well as righteousness, sanctification, and redemption.

1 CORINTHIANS 1:26-30 HCSB

1. According to 1 Corinthians 1:26-30, what kind of people does God choose to using for His rescue mission in our world? What turns people like us into heroes (verse 30)?

64:8 Lord, You are our Father; we are the clay, and You are our potter; we all are the work of Your hands. 45:9 "Woe to the one who argues with his Maker—one clay pot among many. Does clay say to the one forming it: What are you making? Or does your work [say]: He has no hands?

ISAIAH 64:8; 45:9 HCSB

2. What do you think God is saying about you in Isaiah 64 and 45? Why do many of us struggle to accept who we are?

God has an adventure waiting for us as we begin to accept and appreciate who we really are and who He really is. The villain in our story continues to feed us lies about God's goodness, and also about our value to God. He wants to keep us enslave and ineffective. But we're now wise to this scheme; we know the truth – that Jesus brings incredible hope to all of us who are hurting or being held captive.

1 The Spirit of the Sovereign Lord is upon me to preach good news to the poor. He sent me to bind up the brokenhearted, to proclaim freedom for the captives and release from darkness for the prisoners, 2 to proclaim the year of the Lord's favor and the day of vengeance of our God, to comfort all who mourn, 3 to provide for those who grieve in Zion—to bestow on them the crown of beauty instead of ashes, the oil of gladness instead of mourning, and a garment of praise instead of a spirit of despair.

1 ISAIAH 61:1-3 HCSB

3. Which of these characteristics described you when you joined this group? What words of hope and promise in Isaiah 61:1-3 resonate with your heart now?
   - ❏ Poor
   - ❏ Brokenhearted
   - ❏ Captive
   - ❏ Imprisoned in darkness
   - ❏ Mourning
   - ❏ Despairing

4. How do you feel about being invited by Jesus to play a unique role in sharing this incredible news of freedom and redemption with others?

Still More ...

As you step outside yourself to engage in the larger story, you must realize that completing the first pass through the 12 steps doesn't mean there's nothing more for you. Here's some of what God has in store for you as you continue with Him:

I [God] will restore the years that the swarming locust has eaten, the crawling locust, the consuming locust, and the chewing locust.

JOEL 2:25 NKJV

In this passage, locusts represent the torment or consequences that have come into our lives as a result of bad decisions we or other people have made. In our case, they clearly represent the addictions that have chewed up our lives and relationships. Locusts are ravenous, devouring life as they swarm.

5. What does God promise in Joel 2:25 that He will do with your life? What degree of restoration does He describe? How much do you think is possible?

16 I pray that out of his glorious riches he may strengthen you with power through his Spirit in your inner being, 17 so that Christ may dwell in your hearts through faith. And I pray that you, being rooted and established in love, 18 may have power together with all the saints , to grasp how wide and long and high and deep is the love of Christ, 19 and to know this love that surpasses knowledge—that you may be filled to the measure of all the fullness of God. 20 Now to him who is able to do immeasurably than all we ask of imagine, according to his power that is at work within us. 21 to him be glory ...

EPHESIANS 3:16-21 NIV

7 We speak of God's secret wisdom, a wisdom that has been hidden and that God destined for our glory before time began. ... 9 as it is written: "No eye has seen, no ear has heard, no mind has conceived what God has prepared for those who love him."

1 CORINTHIANS 2:7,9 NIV)

6. Read carefully through Ephesians 3:16-21 and 1 Corinthians 2:7,9. List all of the incredible things God has for you now and in eternity

7. How much more do you think God has for you now? How much more as you continue to merge your story with His story?

EMBRACING THE TRUTH - 20 MINUTES

SETTING CAPTIVES FREE

As you join with Jesus in His mission to bind up the brokenhearted, set captives free, and replace beauty for ashes, you won't believe how exciting and deeply fulfilling that can be!

[3] *Blessed be the God and Father of our Lord Jesus Christ, the Father of mercies and the God of all comfort.* [4] *He comforts us in all our affliction, so that we may be able to comfort those who are in any kind of affliction, through the comfort we ourselves receive from God.* [5] *For as the sufferings of Christ overflow to us, so our comfort overflows through Christ.*

2 CORINTHIANS 1:3-5 HCSB

[14] *But thanks be to God, who always leads us in triumph in Christ, and manifests through us the sweet aroma of the knowledge of Him in every place.* [15] *For we are a fragrance of Christ to God among those who are being saved and among those who are perishing;* [16] *to the one an aroma from death to death, to the other an aroma from life to life. And who is adequate for these things?*

2 CORINTHIANS 2:14-16 HCSB

1. How is God the Father portrayed in 2 Corinthians 1:3 and 2:14? How does this portrayal compare to your deepest heart-beliefs about God?

2. How do you think your past wounds and brokenness enhance your usefulness to God in His work of comforting, healing, and setting captives free (2 Corinthians 1:4-5)?

3. What is the world-changing challenge placed before us in 2 Corinthians 2:15-16? How would you answer Paul's question: "Who is adequate for these things?"

4. Look again at these two passages from the perspective of what you receive, rather than what you give. What are the benefits to your own recovery and healing as you share with others, and become God's "triumph" and "sweet aroma" (2 Corinthians 1:4-5 and 15-16)?

The amazing thing is that as you work with Jesus in setting captives free, you find that one of the captives that's becoming more and more free is you! God has made some amazing promises to us if we are willing to raise our eyes to Him (above our current pain) and embrace the larger story. These promises give powerful incentive not to give up, but to continue on to still more ...

LEADER NOTE: *This would be a good time to suggest to the group that redemptive community has had time to take root in your meetings together. Remind them that their journeys are only beginning. Ask the group if they would consider keeping the group together for continued support and redemption. Pass around 3 x 5" cards so people can jot down their potential interest. Some of the group members may be open to the idea.*

Additionally, encourage group members to join the next Stop the Madness *group, either to go through the process again at a deeper level, or to take to an active role in helping to lead the group as a mentor, small-group facilitator, accountability partner, some other that fits you well (discuss the potential with your group facilitator.*

If there are not enough to form a small group, refer these people to your pastor to connect them with a group. If you form a group that does not want to go through Stop the Madness *again, we suggest your next step would be to go through the Serendipity House study entitled* Great Beginnings. *You may order this online at www.SerendipityHouse.com.*

CONNECTING - 20 MINUTES

LEADER: *Use this "Connecting" time to help group members to discuss reservations about this step of sharing our story of redemption with others, then to solidify commitments .*

LET'S GO FOR IT!

1. How ready and willing do you feel about the adventure of setting captives free? What reservations do you have?

2. What unique gifts, talents, resources, and life experience has God given you that you could use for helping to comfort hurting people, to release people from bondage, or to show people the way to Jesus so they can find redemption for their shame and failures?

3. What kind of responses might people have if you encourage them that there is a way out of their problems, pain, and destructive behaviors?

¹³ *Who is there to harm you if you prove zealous for what is good?* ¹⁴ *But even if you should suffer for the sake of righteousness, you are blessed. And do not fear their intimidation, and do not be troubled,* ¹⁵ *but sanctify [or set apart] Christ as Lord in your hearts, always being ready to make a defense [or explanation] to everyone who asks you to give an account for the hope that is in you, yet with gentleness and reverence.*

1 PETER 3:13-15 HCSB

4. Why should we be "zealous"? How do we get ready to "give an account" (verses 14-15)?

5. Who do you know that is struggling and needs some of the overflow of the comfort and new life you are receiving from God? What are you personally willing to do to bring comfort and hope to that person? How about as a group?

LEADER PRAYER OPTION: *Page 4 shows a music CD: Pursued by God: Redemptive Worship Volume 1 from Serendipity House. In place of your group prayer time, you may want to play either the song "I Worship You/More" or "Royalty" from that CD. Download lyrics from www.SerendipityHouse.com/Community (under Group Leaders - Practical Tools). Ask group members to close their eyes and listen, and then at the end of the song privately respond back to God.*

MY PRAYER REQUESTS:

MY GROUP'S PRAYER REQUESTS:

TAKING IT HOME

A QUESTION TO TAKE TO MY HEART:

Read the article "I Stand at the Door" that begins on the next page, and then ask this question of your heart.

 ✳ How willing am I really to "stand at the door" for people? What is it that's driving my hesitancy, indifference, or even possibly my eagerness?

I Stand by the Door*

By Sam Shoemaker, who helped draft the 12 Steps of A.A.

I stand by the door.
I neither go too far in, nor stay too far out,
The door is the most important door in the world-
It is the door through which people walk when they find God.
There's no use my going way inside, and staying there,
When so many are still outside and they, as much as I,
Crave to know where the door is.
And all that so many ever find
Is only the wall where a door ought to be.
They creep along the wall like blind people,
With outstretched, groping hands.
Feeling for a door, knowing there must be a door,
Yet they never find it ...
So I stand by the door.

The most tremendous thing in the world
Is for people to find that door—the door to God.
The most important thing any person can do
Is to take hold of one of those blind, groping hands,
And put it on the latch—the latch that only clicks
And opens to the person's own touch.
People die outside that door, as starving beggars die
On cold nights in cruel cities in the dead of winter—
Die for want of what is within their grasp.
They live, on the other side of it—live because they have not found it.
Nothing else matters compared to helping them find it,
And open it, and walk in, and find Him ...
So I stand by the door.

Go in, great saints, go all the way in—
Go way down into the cavernous cellars,
And way up into the spacious attics—
It is a vast roomy house, this house where God is.
Go into the deepest of hidden casements,
Of withdrawal, of silence, of sainthood.
Some must inhabit those inner rooms.
And know the depths and heights of God,
And call outside to the rest of us how wonderful it is.
Sometimes I take a deeper look in,
Sometimes venture in a little farther;
But my place seems closer to the opening ...
So I stand by the door.

There is another reason why I stand there.
Some people get part way in and become afraid
Lest God and the zeal of His house devour them
For God is so very great, and asks all of us.
And these people feel a cosmic claustrophobia,
And want to get out. "Let me out!" they cry,
And the people way inside only terrify, them more.
Somebody must be by the door to tell them that they are spoiled
For the old life, they have seen too much:
Once taste God, and nothing but God will do any more.
Somebody must be watching for the frightened
Who seek to sneak out just where they came in,
To tell them how much better it is inside.
The people too far in do not see how near these are
To leaving—preoccupied with the wonder of it all.
Somebody must watch for those who have entered the door,
But would like to run away. So for them, too,
I stand by the door.

I admire the people who go way in.
But I wish they would not forget how it was
Before they got in. Then they would be able to help
The people who have not, yet even found the door,
Or the people who want to run away again from God,
You can go in too deeply, and stay in too long,
And forget the people outside the door.
As for me, I shall take my old accustomed place,
Near enough to God to hear Him, and know He is there,
But not so far from people as not to hear them,
And remember they are there, too.
Where? Outside the door—
Thousands of them, millions of them.
But—more important for me—
One of them, two of them, ten of them,
Whose hands I am intended to put on the latch.
So I shall stand by the door and wait
For those who seek it.
"I had rather be a door-keeper ..."
So I stand by the door.

Sam Shoemaker, founder of Faith At Work at Calvary Episcopal Church in New York City, in 1926, was also one of the spiritual leaders who helped draft the 12 Steps of A.A.

* "I Stand By the Door" accessed from www.faithatwork.com on 3/30/06 (Faith@Work™).
  Used by permission.

REQUIRED SUPPLIES AND PREPARATION
FOR EACH SESSION

This section lists the supplies required for the Group Experiences or Listening Prayer Exercises in each session of the study. Preparations instructions provided here for the experiences are also given within each session at the point of use.

INTRODUCTORY SESSION: A LOOK AT THE PATHWAY TO HEALING

Supplies: - Disney-animated movie *The Lion King* on DVD

           - TV/Screen and DVD system

           - Rope with several knots to use an illustration

Preparation: Before the Introductory Session, queue up Scene 19 (runs from 1:03:00 to 1:09:14 minutes) on the DVD.

SESSION 1: WE CAN'T DO IT ON OUR OWN

Supplies: - A large green BLOB – children's modeling clay or putty

Preparation: Create a very large, moldable green BLOB that will be passed around to each member of the group. You may choose to give each group member their own BLOB; this could be modeling clay or a "stress ball."

SESSION 2: HOPE TO STOP THE MADNESS

Supplies: - Peaceful background music – You may use Serendipity House's CD entitled Pursued by God: Redemptive Worship Volume 1, or select your own music

           - Audio system or CD player

Preparation: You're going to lead the group in a short time of listening prayer. Before Session 2, set up your audio system, and search for the light controls and "personal areas" in your meeting space.

SESSION 3: THE POWER TO CHOOSE ... USE IT!

Supplies: - Movie *Indiana Jones and the Last Crusade* on DVD

           - TV/Screen and DVD system

Preparation: Before Session 3, queue up clip toward the end of Scene 33 and let it run into Scene 34 (runs from 1:42:27 to 1:49:08 minutes) on the DVD.

SESSION 4: THE DNA OF OUR ADDICTIONS

Supplies:
- A spiral notebook for each group member (bring extras for any new people)
- Pens or pencil for each group member
- Peaceful background music – You may use Serendipity House's CD entitled Pursued by God: Redemptive Worship Volume 1, or select your own music
- Audio system or CD player
- <u>OPTIONAL</u>: Poster board or large paper to display "top ten" list

Preparation: There's an individual writing activity to get group members into the swing of writing for Step 4 to develop their own personal inventories. Be sure to set up your audio system for the background music.

SESSION 5: BREAK THE POWER OF SECRECY

Supplies:
- Movie *The Goonies* on DVD
- TV/Screen and DVD system
- Poster boards and colored markers for each group member

Preparation: Clip 1 – Before Session 5, queue up the first clip toward the middle of Scene 17 (runs from 51:54 to 52:49 minutes) on the DVD. In this first clip, little chubby Chunk starts into a true confessions time.

Clip 2 – Chunk hilariously wraps up his confession in a second clip at the start of Scene 20 (runs from 58:09 to 59:20 minutes) on the DVD.

Map – Create your own "Story-Telling Map" before Session 5 as an example. See the Group Experience in the "Connecting" segment. Make it strong, but keep it simple.

SESSION 6: NEW THINGS HAVE COME!

Supplies:
- Movie *Star Wars Episode VI: Return of the Jedi* on DVD
- TV/Screen and DVD system

Preparation: Clip 1 – Before Session 6, queue up the first clip in Scenes 43 (runs from 1:55:02 to 1:57:43 minutes) on the DVD. In this clip, Luke makes one last effort to pull his father, Darth Vader, back from the "Dark Side."

Clip 2 – Vader's redemption occurs in Scenes 44 and 45 (runs from 1:59:28 to 2:01:40 minutes) on the

Session 7: A Change of Heart and Mind

Supplies: - A tub or bucket filled with water

              - Dissolvo® paper from a magic supply store or Web site

              - Markers to write on the Dissolvo® paper

              - Peaceful background music — You may use Serendipity House's CD entitled *Pursued by God: Redemptive Worship Volume 1,* or select your own music

              - Audio system or CD player

Preparation: Go to a local magic supply store or one of the following Web sites to purchase Dissolvo® paper. Cut the sheets of paper into small strips that you can pass out to group members. Web sites: www.gospelmagic.com OR www.ronjo.com OR www.dissolvo.com (look under creative products).

Session 8: In Harm's Way

Supplies: - Movie *Meet the Parents* on DVD

              - TV/Screen and DVD system

Preparation: Before Session 8, queue up the clip in the first half of Scene 12 (runs from 59:00 to 1:01:18 minutes) on the DVD. Offense fly during this game of water volleyball.

Session 9: Getting Beyond Regrets - No supplies required

Session 10: Relapse Prevention

Supplies: - Disney-animated movie *The Hunchback of Notre Dame* on DVD

              - TV/Screen and DVD system

Preparation: Clip 1 — Before Session 10, queue up the first clip in the first half of Scene 9 (runs from 27:27 to 30:08 minutes) on the DVD. In this first clip, Quasimodo is freed by Esmeralda.

            Clip 2 — This second clip is used later in Session 10. This clip shows the battle against evil and prisoners being set free. This clip at the start of Scene 24 (runs from 1:12:56 to 1:16:13 minutes) on the DVD.

SESSION 11: KEEPING GOD IN MY STORY

Supplies: - Peaceful background music – You may use Serendipity House's CD entitled Pursued by God: Redemptive Worship Volume 1, or select your own music

              - Audio system or CD player

              - <u>OPTIONAL</u>: Product FLOOD Volume 2 Kit OR FLOOD Volume 2 DVD-A (available from Serendipity House) - Either product contain a powerful short film called "Unforced Rhythms," that's based on Matthew 11:28-30.
(You'll need a DVD/Video system if you use this short film.)

Preparation: You're going to lead the group in a short time of listening prayer. Before Session 11, set up your audio system, and search for the light controls and "personal areas" in your meeting space.

SESSION 12: SETTING CAPTIVES FREE

Supplies: - DreamWorks-animated movie *Shrek* (the original movie) on DVD

              - TV/Screen and DVD system

              - 3 x 5" index cards for <u>each group member</u>

Preparation: <u>Clip</u> – Before Session 812 queue up the clip in the first half of Scene 6 (runs from 26:17 to 28:21 minutes) on the DVD. Shrek explains to Donkey that ogres are like onions.

           <u>Future of Group</u> – Plan in advance of your last meeting a few options for continuation of the group.
(See details near the end of Session 12 in the "LEADER NOTE" box.)

Leading a Successful Small Group

You will find a great deal of helpful information in this section that will be crucial for success as you lead your group.

Reading through this and utilizing the suggested principles and practices will greatly enhance the group experience. You need to accept the limitations of leadership. You cannot transform a life. You must lead your group to the Bible, the Holy Spirit, and the power of Christian community. By doing so your group will have all the tools necessary to walk through the grieving process and embrace life and hope on the other side. The grief process normally lasts longer than eight weeks. But the connections that are built and the truths learned with allow your group members to move toward wholeness.

Make the following things available at each session
- *Stop the Madness: Finding Freedom from Addictions* book for each attendee
- Bible for each attendee
- Boxes of tissue
- Snacks and refreshments
- Dark chocolates
- Pens or pencils for each attendee

Most every session will demand other items be available. Check the list and make sure you have what is needed for each session.

The Setting

General Tips:

1. Prepare for each meeting by reviewing the material, praying for each group member, asking the Holy Spirit to join you at each meeting, and making Jesus the centerpiece of every experience.

2. Create the right environment by making sure chairs are arranged so each person can see the eyes of every other attendee. Set the room temperature at 69 degrees. Make sure pets are in a location where they cannot interrupt the meeting. Request that cell phones are turned off unless someone is expecting an emergency call. Have music playing as people arrive (volume low enough for people to converse) and, if possible, burn a sweet-smelling candle.

3. Try to have soft drinks and coffee available for early arrivals.

4. Have someone with the spiritual gift of hospitality ready to make any new attendees feel welcome.

5. Be sure there is adequate lighting so that everyone can read without straining.

6. There are four types of questions used in each session: Observation (What is the passage telling us?), Interpretation (What does the passage mean?), Self-revelation (How am I doing in light of the truth unveiled?), and Application (Now that I know what I know, what will I do to integrate this truth into my life?). You won't be able to use all the questions in each study, but be sure to use some from each of these types of questions.

7. Connect with group members away from group time. The amount of participation you have during your group meetings is directly related to the amount of time you connect with your group members away from the meeting time.

8. Don't get impatient about the depth of relationship group members are experiencing. Building real Christian Community takes time.

9. Be sure pens and/or pencils are available for attendees at each meeting.

10. Never ask someone to pray aloud without first getting their permission.

Every Meeting:

1. Before the icebreakers, do not say, "Now we're going to do an icebreaker." The meeting should feel like a conversation from beginning to end, not a classroom experience.

2. Be certain every member responds to the icebreaker questions. The goal is for every person to hear his or her own voice early in the meeting. People will then feel comfortable to converse later on. If members can't think of a response, let them know you'll come back to them after the others have spoken.

3. Remember, a great group leader talks less than 10% of the time. If you ask a question and no one answers, just wait. If you create an environment where you fill the gaps of silence, the group will quickly learn they needn't join you in the conversation.

4. Don't be hesitant to call people by name as you ask them to respond to questions or to give their opinions. Be sensitive, but engage everyone in the conversation.

5. Don't ask people to read aloud unless you have gotten their permission prior to the meeting. Feel free to ask for volunteers to read.

The Group

Each small group has it's own persona. Every group is made up of a unique set of personalities, backgrounds, and life experiences. This diversity creates a dynamic distinctive to that specific group of people. Embracing the unique character of your group and the individual's in that group is vital to group members experiencing all you're hoping for.

Treat each person as special, responsible, and valuable members of this Christian community. By doing so you'll bring out the best in each of them thus creating a living, breathing, life-changing group dynamic.

NOTE: Because this study is designed as an integrated whole, with each session building on the previous sessions, you will not want to consider your sessions open to new members once you get rolling. This will also help to help group members open up as they develop trust in each other over time. Invite people that want to join the group part way through to join the next group that forms.

Support Roles

Many of your group members will feel that we've been to hell and back, and they long for someone and need others to guide them to safer, more appropriate places. Following are some key support roles that you need to consider:

Facilitator (Group Leader): This person helps the group stay on track. It's best if this person has already been through this or another recovery process. NOTE: Be sure to enlist an Assistant or Co-facilitator. This person can support the Facilitator in a variety of ways, and can lead the group sessions if the Facilitator is unable to make a meeting. This is a great way to train future group leaders.

Mentors: Try to enlist people that have experienced successful recovery from some addiction to act as mentors to group members. It is not necessary that Mentors attend every meeting, but they should join in at least periodically. Mentors can assist more than one person if they feel they have time and energy. Mentors must commit to calling their group members at least once each week, as well as get together in person at least every other week. Mentors can provide encouragement, perspective, and the counsel of experience. NOTE: Choose dependable and wise people for this role. You should just assign mentors to group members after the first meeting or two.

Accountability Partners: Regularly encourage group members to seek out their own Accountability Partner(s)—someone who will encourage and challenge them. Don't underestimate the powerful influence of another person fighting through the process. Encourage Accountability Partners to meet weekly over lunch. They will need ask tough questions, encourage each other, and help each other think more objectively. Accountability Partners must be the same gender, unless someone is struggling with homosexuality. NOTE: It may be advisable for group members to select an Accountability Partner from within the group, but an outside person is fine too. The key point is that there must be a level of trust and openness.

The Holy Spirit: Unless the Spirit of God shows up and meets with you in each session group members will only gain information. Life change and healing is the goal. Be sure to spend time each week praying for your group. Enlist a prayer support team; you're going to be in some heavy spiritual battles! As we invite God into this process, He *will* respond and guide group members into truth, and that truth is vital to healing and freedom (John 8:32)!

What Can You Do?

Support — Provide plenty of time for support among the group members. Encourage members to connect with each other between meetings when necessary. Some examples are:
a) taking a call any time of day whenever another group member is struggling with temptation
b) coping with the side effects of treatment
c) instructing in how to look for a job
d) instructing in how to apply for financial assistance
e) helping in practical ways

Shared Feelings — Reassure the members how normal their feelings are; even if relief and sadness are mixed together. Encourage the members to share their feelings with one another.

Advice Giving — Avoid giving advice. Encourage cross-talk (members talking to each other), but limit advice giving. Should and ought to statements tend to increase the guilt the loss has already created.

Silence — Silence is not a problem. Even though it may seem awkward, silence is just a sign that people are not ready to talk. It DOES NOT mean they aren't thinking or feeling. If the silence needs to be broken, be sure you break it with the desire to move forward.

Prayer – Prayer is vital to healing. Starting and ending with prayer is important. However, people may need prayer in the middle of the session. Here's a way to know when the time is right to pray. If a member is sharing and you sense a need to pray, then begin to look for a place to add it.

Feelings vs. Right Choices and Thinking – There may be a temptation to overemphasize feelings rather that choices and thinking. It is important that you keep the focus on moving forward regardless of how we feel. Our feelings may make the journey slow, but left to feelings only, progress will shut down.

As you move toward the end of the study, be aware that it is a bittersweet time for the group. It will be painful for them to say goodbye to one another. Set a time for the group to have a reunion.

ACKNOWLEDGMENTS

This project was a true team effort. We wish to thank the team that labored to make this life-changing small-group experience a reality.

Written by: Ben Colter and Dr. Paul Hardy

Special thanks Ron Keck for permitting us to use his "Captive Heart Model" and "Critical Path to Healing" construct in this study

Editorial team: Ron Keck, Lori Mayes, Sarah Hogg and Jenna Anderson

Art direction: Scott Lee of Scott Lee Designs

Cover and interior design: Roy Roper of Wideyedesign

Meeting Planner

The leader or facilitator of our group is _____ .
The apprentice facilitator for this group is _____ .

We will meet on the following dates and times:

	Date	Day	Time
Intro Session	_____	_____	_____
Session 1	_____	_____	_____
Session 2	_____	_____	_____
Session 3	_____	_____	_____
Session 4	_____	_____	_____
Session 5	_____	_____	_____
Session 6	_____	_____	_____
Session 7	_____	_____	_____
Session 8	_____	_____	_____
Session 9	_____	_____	_____
Session 10	_____	_____	_____
Session 11	_____	_____	_____
Session 12	_____	_____	_____

We will meet at:

Intro	_____
Session 1	_____
Session 2	_____
Session 3	_____
Session 4	_____
Session 5	_____
Session 6	_____
Session 7	_____
Session 8	_____
Session 9	_____
Session 10	_____
Session 11	_____
Session 12	_____

Refreshments and/or child-care will be arranged by:

Session 1	_____
Session 2	_____
Session 3	_____
Session 4	_____
Session 5	_____
Session 6	_____
Session 7	_____
Session 8	_____
Session 9	_____
Session 10	_____
Session 11	_____
Session 12	_____

Welcome to Community!

Meeting together with a group of people to study God's Word and experience life together is an exciting adventure.

A small group is ... *a group of people unwilling to settle for anything less than redemptive community.*

Core Values

Community:

God is relational, so He created us to live in relationship with Him and each other. Authentic community involves sharing life together and connecting on many levels with the people in our group.

Group Process:

Developing authentic community requires a step-by-step process. It's a journey of sharing our stories with each other and learning together.

Stages of Development:

Every healthy group goes through various stages as it matures over a period of months or years. We begin with the birth of a new group, deepen our relationships in the growth and development stages, and ultimately multiply to form other new groups.

Interactive Bible Study:

God provided the Bible as an instruction manual of life. We need to deepen our understanding of God's Word. People learn and remember more as they wrestle with truth and learn from others. The process of Bible discovery and group interaction will enhance our growth.

EXPERIENTIAL GROWTH:

The goal of studying the Bible together is not merely a quest for knowledge, but should result in real life change. Beyond solely reading, studying, and dissecting the Bible, being a disciple of Christ involves reunifying knowledge with experience. We do this by bringing our questions to God, opening a dialogue with our hearts (instead of killing our desires), and utilizing other ways to listen to God speak to us (group interaction, nature, art, movies, circumstances, etc.). Experiential growth is always grounded in the Bible as God's primary means of revelation and our ultimate truth-source.

THE POWER OF GOD:

Our processes and strategies will be ineffective unless we invite and embrace the presence and power of God. In order to experience community and growth, Jesus needs to be the centerpiece of our group experiences and the Holy Spirit must be at work.

REDEMPTIVE COMMUNITY:

Healing occurs best within the context of community and relationships. A key aspect of our spiritual development and journey through grief and pain is seeing ourselves through the eyes of others, sharing our stories, and ultimately being set free from the secrets and lies we embrace that enslave our souls.

MISSION:

God has invited us into a larger story with a great mission. It is a mission that involves setting captives free and healing the broken-hearted (Isaiah 61:1-2). However, we can only join in this mission to the degree that we've let Jesus bind up our wounds and set us free. As a group experiences true redemptive community, other people will be attracted to that group, and through that group to Jesus. We should be alert to other people that we can invite when a new group is getting ready to start up.

STAGES OF GROUP LIFE

Each healthy small group will move through various stages as it matures. There is no prescribed time frame for moving through these stages because each group is unique.

BIRTH STAGE: This is the time in which group members form relationships and begin to develop community.

MULTIPLY STAGE: The group begins the multiplication process. Members pray about their involvement in establishing new groups. The new groups begin the cycle again with the Birth Stage.

GROWTH STAGE: Here the group members begin to care for one another as they learn what it means to apply what they have discovered through Bible study, shared experiences, worship, and prayer

DEVELOP STAGE: The Bible study and shared experiences deepen while the group members develop their gifts and skills. The group explores ways to invite neighbors, friends, and coworkers to meetings.

SUBGROUPING: If you have more than 12 people at a meeting, Serendipity House recommends dividing into smaller subgroups after the "Breaking the Ice" segment. Ask one person to be the leader of each subgroup, following the "Leader" directions for the session. The Group Leader should bring the subgroups back together for the closing. Subgrouping is also very useful when more openness and intimacy is required. The "Connecting" segment in each session is a great time to divide into smaller groups of 4 to 6 people.

Sharing Your Stories

The sessions in *Stop the Madness* are designed to help you share some of your personal lives with the people in your group as you learn to walk through your grief and embrace God's hope. Through your time together, each member of the group is encouraged to move from low risk, less personal sharing to higher risk communication. Real community will not develop apart from increasing intimacy of the group over time.

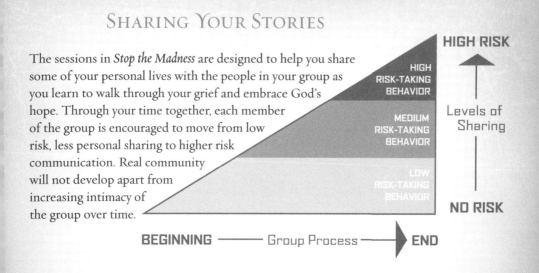

Sharing Your Lives

As you share your lives together during this time, it is important to recognize that it is God who has brought each person to this group, gifting the individuals to play a vital role in the group (1 Corinthians 12:1). Each of you was uniquely designed to contribute in your own unique way to building into the lives of the other people in your group. As you get to know one another better, consider the following four areas that will be unique for each person. These areas will help you get a "grip" how you can better support others and how they can support you.

G – SPIRITUAL GIFTS: God has given you unique spiritual gifts
(1 Corinthians 12; Romans 12:3-8; Ephesians 4:1-16; etc.)

R – RESOURCES: You have resources that perhaps only you can share, including skill, abilities, possessions, money, and time
(Acts 2:44-47; Ecclesiastes 4:9-12, etc.)

I – INDIVIDUAL EXPERIENCES: You have past experiences, both good and bad, that God can use to strengthen others
(2 Corinthians 1:3-7; Romans 8:28, etc.)

P – PASSIONS: There are things that excite and motivate you. God has given you those desires and passions to use for His purposes
(Psalm 37:4,23; Proverbs 3:5-6,13-18; etc.)

To better understand how a group should function and develop in these four areas, consider going through the Serendipity House study entitled *Great Beginnings*.

Group Directory

Write your name on this page. Pass your books around and ask your group members to fill in their names and contact information (as each is comfortable) in each other's books.

Your Name: _____

Name: _____	Name: _____
Address: _____	Address: _____
City: _____	City: _____
Zip Code: _____	Zip Code: _____
Home Phone: _____	Home Phone: _____
Mobile Phone: _____	Mobile Phone: _____
E-mail: _____	E-mail: _____
Name: _____	Name: _____
Address: _____	Address: _____
City: _____	City: _____
Zip Code: _____	Zip Code: _____
Home Phone: _____	Home Phone: _____
Mobile Phone: _____	Mobile Phone: _____
E-mail: _____	E-mail: _____
Name: _____	Name: _____
Address: _____	Address: _____
City: _____	City: _____
Zip Code: _____	Zip Code: _____
Home Phone: _____	Home Phone: _____
Mobile Phone: _____	Mobile Phone: _____
E-mail: _____	E-mail: _____
Name: _____	Name: _____
Address: _____	Address: _____
City: _____	City: _____
Zip Code: _____	Zip Code: _____
Home Phone: _____	Home Phone: _____
Mobile Phone. _____	Mobile Phone: _____
E-mail: _____	E-mail: _____
Name: _____	Name: _____
Address: _____	Address: _____
City: _____	City: _____
Zip Code: _____	Zip Code: _____
Home Phone: _____	Home Phone: _____
Mobile Phone: _____	Mobile Phone: _____
E-mail: _____	E-mail: _____